A Manual for Bishops

Rights and Responsibilities of

Diocesan Bishops in the

Revised Code of Canon Law

Revised Edition

National Conference of Catholic Bishops

A Manual for Bishops was first published by the National Conference of Catholic Bishops in May 1983 at the request of the Canonical Affairs Committee. Since that time, over 3000 copies of the publication have been distributed and the Conference continues to receive requests for additional copies. In 1991 *Revisions to A Manual for Bishops* was published updating the material in accord with changes or clarifications in canonical legislation on the rights and responsibilities of the diocesan bishop. *A Manual for Bishops—Revised Edition* follows the 1983 schematic organization, incorporating the 1991 revisions prepared by Father Thomas J. Green, professor of canon law at The Catholic University of America and author of the 1983 text. The revised document is presented in a new format, deleting the section entitled "Special Legislation" which is now contained in *Complementary Norms* published in 1991. *A Manual for Bishops—Revised Edition* is authorized for publication by the undersigned.

Monsignor Robert N. Lynch
General Secretary
February 24, 1992   NCCB/USCC

ISBN 1-55586-496-1

Contents

I. Introduction

The revised Code of Canon Law greatly emphasizes the exercise of the leadership role of the diocesan bishop within the particular church. The law restates the conciliar teaching that episcopal consecration confers the offices of teaching and ruling along with the office of sanctifying. The diocesan bishop (as distinct from the coadjutor or the auxiliary bishop) is viewed as the leader of a sacramental community called to pursue a multifaceted mission (kerygma, koinonia, diakonia). He is to be a key principle of unity in catalyzing its ministerial resources for increasingly more effective service in and for the world. For the mission of the Church is not the sole prerogative of the bishop and the clergy. Rather, he is to foster the involvement of a broad cross section of the People of God in this missionary enterprise.

The extensive scope and complexity of this episcopal leadership role is evident from the fact that there are nearly 500 references to the episcopal office in the revised Code. Accordingly some effort should be made to clarify somewhat succinctly certain significant aspects of that office in terms of several general themes. That is the purpose of this manual. It is hoped that it may help bishops and those working closely with them in the daily exercise of their varied responsibilities for the good of the People of God.

This manual is no substitute for a careful reading of and reflecting on the revised Code in light of pertinent commentaries. In fact its intelligent use presupposes continual access to the text of the revised Code, key points of which the manual attempts to express succinctly. A schematic presentation, such as the manual, cannot do justice to the comprehensiveness of the revised Code or its theological-canonical sources.

The manual is also no substitute for theological-pastoral reflection on the episcopal office. As significant as the revised

Code is, it is certainly not a theological-pastoral commentary on the office of bishop; this is all the more true for the manual. In this connection the reader might consult conciliar documents such as *Lumen gentium* and *Christus Dominus* and curial documents such as the *Directory on the Pastoral Ministry of Bishops*. Only within a broad theological-pastoral horizon can the individual canons referred to be responsibly interpreted.

The following references to the revised Code are organized according to two main headings: (1) the bishop's sanctifying, teaching and governing ministries and (2) his relationship to various groups of people in the diocese: laity, clergy, religious and those not fully in communion with the Catholic Church. Any arrangement of such an extensive and complex amount of material is necessarily somewhat artificial. However, the above mentioned general headings seem to be reasonably useful and faithful to the structuring of material in the conciliar and curial documents referred to in the preceding paragraph.

Most of the subsequent material is further distinguished in terms of whether the bishop is exercising a certain right or being bound by a certain responsibility. When reference is made to *rights* in these citations, it does not always mean that the canon uses the technical Latin term *ius*. If this is the case, *ius* will be placed in parentheses at the end of the reference. Generally such canons refer to various areas in which the bishop is legally competent and may exercise certain prerogatives.

At times the bishop both may enjoy a certain prerogative and be bound by an obligation in a given area. Hence it is advisable to consult both the section on rights and that on responsibilities for a proper understanding of the status of the bishop on a given issue.

At times the canons speak explicitly of the diocesan bishop as such *(episcopus dioecesanus)* as distinct from *local ordinary, ordinary* simply or a comparable expression. In such instances only the diocesan bishop is competent to act in the administrative arena, and others may not act without an explicit mandate. In such cases an asterisk (*) is placed in the margin to the left of the pertinent reference.

Occasionally the manual does not deal directly with the rights and responsibilities of bishops but rather with the legal status of various persons (e.g., vicar general) or institutes (e.g., college of consultors) which play a noteworthy part in the exercise of the episcopal office. Furthermore, at times, references are made not to certain persons or institutes but rather to certain legal points that are particularly relevant to the exercise of the

2

episcopal office, e.g., areas where diocesan legislation is called for and general principles on administrative activity.

The reader will find an index of significant themes at the end of the manual. This should facilitate its use in the service of the pastoral life of the various particular churches.

II. The Bishop's Sanctifying Ministry

> . . . bishops are the principal dispensers of the mysteries of God, just as they are the governors, promoters, and guardians of the entire liturgical life in the church committed to them. . . . 'Intent upon prayer and the ministry of the word' (Acts 6:4), they should devote their labor to this end, that all those committed to their care may be of one mind in prayer and through the reception of the sacraments may grow in grace and be faithful witnesses to the Lord. As those who lead others to perfection, bishops should be diligent in fostering holiness among their clerics, religious, and laity according to the special vocation of each.
>
> *Christus Dominus* 15: Walter M. Abbott, SJ, ed., *Documents of Vatican II*, pp. 406-407

A. The General Canons on the Sanctifying Mission of the Church and on the Sacraments

1. Rights of Bishops

1. Function as high priest, principal dispenser of the mysteries of God and moderator, promoter and guardian of liturgical life (c.835,1)

2. Issue appropriate liturgical norms within limits of his authority (c.838,4)

* 3. Judge 'grave necessity' when Western Christians not in full communion may receive penance, anointing and Eucharist (c.844,4)

4. Consecrate or bless sacred oils (c.847,1)

2. Responsibilities of Bishops

1. Foster sanctity of faithful and especially their active participation in the Church's sacramental life (c.387)

5

2. Celebrate the *Missa pro populo* (c.388)

3. Preside personally at liturgical celebrations (c.389)

4. Be vigilant regarding the authenticity of prayers and other pious practices (c.839,2)

5. Consult leaders of other Christian churches before issuing guidelines on sacramental sharing (c.844,5)

B. Baptism

1. Rights of Bishops

1. Permit baptism in private home for a grave cause (c.860,1)

2. Issue norms on baptisms in hospitals (c.860,2)

3. Function as ordinary minister of baptism (c.861,1)

4. Depute extraordinary minister of baptism (c.861,2)

5. Baptize those over 14 if deemed appropriate (c.863)

6. Determine age other than 16 for sponsor (c.874,1,2°-pastor or minister may also do this by way of exception)

2. Responsibilities of Bishops

Nothing explicit

C. Confirmation

1. Rights of Bishops

1. Consecrate chrism (c.880,2)

2. Function as ordinary minister of confirmation (c.882)

* 3. Empower one or more priests to confirm on a regular basis (c.884,1)

* 4. Associate priests with him in confirming ministry on an *ad hoc* basis (c.884,2)

5. Licitly confirm all in diocese even those not his subjects unless their ordinary objects (c.886,1)

6. Determine age for confirmation other than age of discretion for a serious reason unless conference of bishops has determined the age (c.891)

2. Responsibilities of Bishops

1. Confirm subjects personally or utilize assistance of another bishop (c.884,1)

2. Respond to reasonable request for confirmation (c.885,1)

3. Obtain permission of local ordinary to confirm licitly outside his diocese (c.886,2)

D. Eucharist

1. Rights of Bishops

1. Preside over Eucharistic assembly (c.899,2)
2. Issue celebret for priest to celebrate elsewhere (c.903)
3. Permit bination or trination for a just cause (c.905,2)
4. Function as ordinary minister of the Eucharist (c.910,1)
5. Reserve the Eucharist in his private chapel and authorize its reservation outside parish churches and churches of religious (c.934,1,2°)
6. Issue rules on laypersons' keeping the Eucharist on their persons or taking it with them on a journey (c.935)
7. Depute someone other than an extraordinary minister to preside over exposition/reposition of the Eucharist (c.943)
8. Issue norms to deal with situation when ordinary minister of Eucharistic exposition and benediction is unavailable (c.943)
9. Determine purposes for which more than one stipend may be taken by a priest celebrating the Eucharist more than once a day (c.951,1)
10. Receive surplus Mass obligations (c.956)
11. Be vigilant regarding fulfillment of Mass obligations in churches of secular clergy (c.957) (*ius*)

2. Responsibilities of Bishops

1. Be vigilant re: fulfillment of Mass obligations (c.957)
2. Examine Mass stipend registers each year (c.958,2)

E. Penance

1. Rights of Bishops

* 1. Determine if conditions for general absolution are met in the diocese (c.961,2)
2. Hear confessions anywhere in the world validly, and

licitly as well, unless diocesan bishop elsewhere is unwilling to permit this (c.967,1)

3. Grant confessional faculties (c.969,1)

4. Revoke confessional faculties yet only for a serious reason (c.974,1)

2. Responsibilities of Bishops

1. Act in light of criteria agreed upon by the other members of the conference of bishops if guidelines on general absolution are to be formulated (c.961,2)

2. Consult the ordinary of extern priest before granting confessional faculties (c.971,1)

3. Notify the ordinary of incardination if confessional faculties of one of his priests are revoked (c.974,3)

F. Anointing of the Sick

1. Rights of Bishops

1. Determine norms for communal anointing services (c.1002)

2. Responsibilities of Bishops

Nothing explicit

G. Orders

1. Rights of Bishops

a. Celebration and Minister of Ordination

1. Function as minister of ordination (c.1012)

2. Proper bishop ordains his own subjects or those for whom appropriate dimissorials have been received (c.1015,1-2) (proper bishop = bishop of diocese in which candidate has domicile or in which he intends to minister if it is a case of *diaconal* ordination; in case of *presbyteral* ordination, it is the bishop of the diocese of incardination, which is effected by diaconal ordination—c.1016).

* 3. Issue dimissorials for those candidates subject to him (c.1018,1,1°)

* 4. Send dimissorials to any bishop in communion with Holy See of the same rite as candidate (c.1021)
* 5. Issue dimissorials conditionally and revoke them (c.1023)

b. *Those to Be Ordained*

* 1. Proper bishop judges candidate's aptitude for ordination and usefulness for Church ministry (c.1025,1-2)
* 2. Dispense from minimum age for presbyteral ordination (25 years of age) or diaconal ordination (23 for transitory deacon; 25 for unmarried permanent deacon; 35 for married permanent deacon) as long as the age of the candidate does not exceed the minimum age by more than a year (c.1031,1-2,4)
* 3. Determine time for deacon pastoral internship (c.1032,2)
* 4. Proper bishop admits individual to candidacy (c.1034,1)
* 5. Receive free commitment of candidate to ecclesial service (c.1036)

6. Determine the place and format of five-day retreat before reception of orders (c.1039)

7. Judge that neophyte is sufficiently mature in faith as not to be impeded from receiving orders (c.1042,3^0)

8. Judge that one afflicted with psychic disorder may exercise orders (c.1044,2,2^0)

9. Dispense from irregularities and impediments to orders whose dispensation is not reserved to the Holy See (c.1047,4). Only the following are *reserved to the Holy See*:

> a) Any irregularities if the fact on which they are based has been brought into the judicial arena (c.1047,1)
>
> b) The following *irregularities* as regards the *reception of orders* (c.1047,2,1^0-2^0):
>
> > 1) Public offense of apostasy, heresy or schism (c.1041,2^0)
> >
> > 2) Public attempted marriage by one bound by the impediments of prior bond, sacred orders or a public perpetual vow of chastity or with a woman bound by the impediments of

prior bond or a public perpetual vow of
chastity (c.1041,3⁰)

3) Public or occult offense of voluntary homicide or the procuring of an abortion
(c.1041,4⁰)

c) The following *impediment* to the *reception of orders*: marriage unless one is to be ordained a permanent deacon (cc.1047,1,3⁰; 1042,1⁰)

d) The following *irregularities* as regards the *exercise of orders*: (c.1047,3):

1) Public attempted marriage by one bound
by the impediments of prior bond, sacred orders or a public perpetual vow of chastity or
with a woman bound by the impediments of
prior bond or a public perpetual vow of
chastity (cc.1044,1,3⁰; 1041,3⁰)

2) Public or occult offense of voluntary homicide or the procuring of an abortion
(cc.1044,1,3⁰; 1041,4⁰)

Hence any ordinary may dispense from the following:

a) *Irregularities* as regards the *reception of orders*:

1) Insanity and psychic disorders provided
that the ordinary, after consulting with an
expert, judges that the disorder is cured and
no longer renders a candidate unfit for ministry (c.1041,1⁰)

2) Occult offense of apostasy, heresy or
schism (c.1041,2⁰)

3) Occult attempted marriage by one bound
by the impediments of prior bond, sacred orders or a public perpetual vow of chastity or
with a woman bound by the impediments of
prior bond or a public perpetual vow of
chastity (c.1041,3⁰)

4) Self-mutilation or the mutilation of another or attempted suicide (c.1041,5⁰)

5) A deacon or layperson attempting to posit
an act of orders reserved to bishops or pres-
byters or a presbyter or bishop attempting to
posit such an act despite being prohibited by
a declared or inflicted penalty (c.1041,6⁰)

b) Simple *impediments* to the *reception of orders*:

1) Having an office forbidden to clerics

which demands civil accountability
(c.1042, 2⁰)

    2) Being a neophyte until judged mature by the ordinary (c.1042,3⁰)

c) *Irregularities* as regards the *exercise of orders* (c.1047,3):

    1) Illegitimate reception of orders while subject to an irregularity (c.1044,1,1⁰)

    2) Public offense of apostasy, heresy or schism (c.1044,1,2⁰)

    3) Self-mutilation or the mutilation of another or attempted suicide (c.1041,5⁰)

    4) A deacon or layperson attempting to posit an act of orders reserved to bishops or presbyters or a presbyter or bishop attempting to posit such an act despite being prohibited by a declared or inflicted penalty (c.1041,6⁰)

d) *Simple impediments* to the *exercise of orders* (c.1044,2⁰):

    1) Illegitimate reception of orders while subject to an impediment (c.1044,2,1⁰)

    2) Insanity and psychic disorders provided that the ordinary, after consulting with an expert, permits the exercise of the order (c.1044,2,2⁰)

*10. Use various means besides seminary testimonials in preordination scrutinies (c.1051,2)

c. Registration and Proof of Ordination
Nothing explicit

2. Responsibilities of Bishops

a. Celebration and Minister of Ordination
1. Obtain papal mandate before consecrating bishop (c.1013)

2. Principal consecrator should use at least two other bishops in consecration unless dispensed by Holy See (c.1014)

3. Obtain papal mandate to ordain Oriental candidate (c.1015,2)

4. Obtain permission of local bishop to ordain outside one's own diocese (c.1017)

* 5. Obtain all necessary testimonials and documents

required by canons 1050-1051 before issuing dimissorials (c.1020)

* 6. Obtain papal mandate to send dimissorials to bishop of another rite (c.1021)

* 7. Ordaining bishop to check authenticity of dimissorials (c.1022)

b. Those to Be Ordained

* 8. Ordaining bishop should see to it that his subject ordained for another diocese will indeed serve in it (c.1025,3)

* 9. See to it that candidates for ordination are properly instructed and understand the obligations of the order in question (c.1028)

*10. Ordain only qualified candidates (c.1029)

*11. Needs canonical reason, even if occult, to refuse to ordain a deacon a priest (c.1030)

*12. Needs canonical impediment or other serious reason to prevent deacon refusing priesthood from exercising order (c.1038)

*13. Check on fulfillment of retreat requirement before ordination (c.1039)

14. Consult expert regarding possible exercise of orders by one afflicted with a psychic disorder (c.1044,2,2^0)

*15. Ordaining bishop to see to it that all is in order for ordination, e.g., requisite documents, expediting of scrutinies, positive arguments for ordaining candidate (c.1052,1)

*16. Ordaining bishop not to ordain one whose qualifications are questionable (c.1052,2)

c. Registration and Proof of Ordination

*17. Ordaining bishop to give one ordained a certificate of ordination and notify latter's ordinary if the ordained is not his subject (c.1053,2)

18. Transmit notice of ordination to parish of baptism of candidate (c.1054)

H. Marriage

1. Rights of Bishops

a. Pastoral Care and Preparation for Marriage

1. Authorize the marriage of certain types of persons (c.1071):

a) Migrants

b) Those whose marriages cannot be recognized or celebrated by the state, e.g., undocumented aliens, senior citizens not wanting marriage to be recorded civilly because of Social Security complications

c) Someone who has natural obligations to a former spouse or children

d) Minors whose parents are unaware of or reasonably opposed to the marriage (minors = those under 18)

e) Those entering a marriage by proxy (cf.c.1105)

f) Those under censure

g) Notorious ex-Catholics (canons on mixed marriages operative here—c.1125)

(Mixed marriages also though not explicitly referred to in c.1071 but rather in 1125)

b. *Diriment Impediments in General*

1. Prohibit marriage for a time though not with an invalidating effect (c.1077) (*vetitum*)

2. Dispense from nonreserved impediments (c.1078,1), i.e., from all impediments except:

a) Those of divine law, e.g., impotence, ligamen, consanguinity in direct line or in second degree collateral line (cc.1078,3; 1084; 1085,1; 1091)

b) Sacred orders and public perpetual vow of chastity in an institute of pontifical right (c.1078,2,1°; cc.1087-1088)

c) Conjugicide (cc.1078,2,2°; 1190)

Therefore local ordinaries may dispense from the following impediments:

a) Age (c.1083,1)

b) Disparity of worship (c.1086)

c) Abduction (c.1089)

d) Consanguinity except in the direct line or in the second degree of the collateral line (c.1091)

e) Affinity in the direct line (c.1092)

f) Public propriety (c.1093)

g) Legal relationship based on civil adoption as regards the direct line or the second degree of the collateral line (c.1094)

3. Dispense from canonical form and all ecclesiastical impediments except presbyterate in danger of death (c.1079,1)

4. Dispense from all ecclesiastical impediments except sacred orders and public perpetual vow of chastity in an institute of pontifical right in an *omnia parata* situation, i.e., all prepared for marriage and danger of grave evil if it is deferred until a dispensation is obtained from competent authority (c.1030,1)

c. Diriment Impediments in Particular
Nothing explicit

d. Consent
1. Authorize in writing licit celebration of marriage with a present or past condition (c.1102,3)

e. Canonical Form
1. Witness marriage even of nonsubjects in diocese for validity, as long as one party is Latin rite (cc.1108-1109)

2. Empower priests or deacons to assist validly at marriages even on a general basis even if they're not assigned to a parish (c.1111,1)

* 3. Empower layperson to be official witness at marriage for validity with permission of Holy See and after favorable *votum* of conference of bishops (c.1112,1)

4. Permit marriage elsewhere than in regularly authorized church (parish of either party) (c.1115) even in an appropriate place other than church (c.1118,2)

5. Possibly determine guidelines on registration of marriage (c.1121,1) (conference of bishops also competent)

f. Mixed Marriages
1. Authorize mixed marriages under certain conditions (c.1125)

2. Dispense from form in mixed marriage = right (*ius*) of local ordinary of Catholic party after consulting local ordinary of place where marriage is to be celebrated if it is different from diocese of one granting dispensation from form (c.1127,2) [conference of bishops is to determine norms to regulate such dispensations]

g. Secret Marriage
1. Permit secret marriage under conditions of cc.1131-1133 (c.1130)

h. Effects of Marriage
Nothing explicit

i. Separation of Spouses
Art. 1: Dissolution of Bond
1. Permit interpellations before baptism of convert or possibly dispense from them if they're perceived to be impossible or useless (c.1144,2)
2. Preside over interpellations = local ordinary of convert (c.1145,1)
3. Permit convert utilizing Pauline privilege to marry a non-Catholic (c.1147)
Art. 2: Separation without Dissolution of the Bond
1. Permit conjugal separation for due cause (c.1153,1)

j. Convalidation
Art. 1: Simple Convalidation
Nothing explicit
Art. 2: Sanation
1. Sanate certain marriages unless an impediment of divine or natural law has ceased or dispensation is reserved to the Holy See (c.1165,2)

2. Responsibilities of Bishops

a. Pastoral Care and Preparation for Marriage
1. Care for spiritual enrichment of married persons (c.1063) (general reference to 'pastors of souls')
2. See to organization of pastoral care of married persons with due regard for views of men and women of experience and expertise if deemed appropriate (c.1064)

b. Diriment Impediments in General
Nothing explicit

c. Diriment Impediments in Particular
Nothing explicit

d. Consent
Nothing explicit

e. Canonical Form
Nothing explicit
1. Registration of marriage in a dispensation from form situation (c.1121,3)

f. Mixed Marriages
1. Support those couples in mixed marriages (c.1128)

g. Secret Marriage
1. Maintain obligation of secrecy regarding secret marriage (c.1131,2^0) unless such an obligation ceases for due cause, grave scandal or grave damage to the dignity of marriage (c.1132)

h. Effects of Marriage
Nothing explicit

i. Separation of Spouses
Art. 1: Dissolution of the Bond
1. See to it that polygamist availing self of Pauline privilege provides for needs of dismissed wives (c.1148,3)
Art. 2: Separation without Dissolution of Bond
Nothing explicit

j. Convalidation
Nothing explicit

I. Other Acts of Divine Worship besides Sacraments

1. Rights of Bishops

a. Sacramentals
1. Authorize laity to be ministers of some sacramentals (c.1168)
2. Competent to perform consecrations and blessings some of which are reserved to pope or bishop (c.1169,1-2)
3. Authorize especially qualified priests to perform exorcisms (c.1172)

b. Liturgy of the Hours
Nothing explicit

c. Church Burial

4. Permit Catholic burial service for unbaptized infant or member of other Christian church (c.1183,2-3)

5. Judge appropriateness of Christian burial in doubtful cases (c.1184,2)

d. Cult of the Saints, Sacred Images and Relics

6. Approve in writing restoration of precious images (c.1189)

e. Vows and Oaths

7. Dispense subjects from private vows or delegate others to do so (c.1196,1⁰,3⁰)

2. Responsibilities of Bishops

a. Sacramentals
Nothing explicit

b. Liturgy of the Hours
Nothing explicit

c. Church Burial
Nothing explicit

d. Cult of the Saints, Sacred Images and Relics

1. Consult experts regarding restoration of precious objects (c.1189)

e. Vows and Oaths
Nothing explicit

J. Sacred Places and Times

1. Rights of Bishops

a. Sacred Places

* 1. Competent to dedicate sacred places or delegate another bishop or priest to do so (c.1206)

2. Bless sacred place or delegate priest to do so (c.1207)

3. Bless church (c.1207)

4. Permit secular use of sacred place (c.1210)

5. Judge when sacred place is violated (c.1211)

6. Decree that henceforth a sacred place may be converted to a secular purpose (c.1212)

* 7. Give written consent that a church be built (c.1215,1)

* 8. Approve religious building church even if he has already approved their establishment of a house (c.1215,3)

* 9. Authorize conversion of a church to secular purposes if it cannot be repaired or if other serious reasons suggest such a conversion (c.1222)

10. Permit building of oratory (c.1223)

11. Approve conversion of an oratory to secular purposes (c.1224,2)

12. Forbid certain functions from taking place in an oratory (c.1225)

13. Permit erection of private chapel (c.1226)

14. Build for himself private chapel with same rights as oratory (c.1227)

15. Permit Mass and other sacred functions to take place in a private chapel (c.1227)

16. Permit erection of shrine (c.1230)

17. Approve statutes of diocesan shrine (c.1232,1)

18. Approve establishment of cemeteries in cases other than parishes or religious institute houses (c.1241,2)

b. Sacred Times

* 1. Determine feast days or penitential days on an individual basis or *per modum actus* (c.1244,2)

2. Determine norms for pastors' dispensing subjects regarding feast days and penitential days (c.1245)

3. Determine norms regarding the liturgy of the word in situations where normal Eucharistic participation is impossible (c.1248,2)

2. Responsibilities of Bishops

a. Sacred Places

* 1. Hear presbyteral council and neighboring rectors before approving the building of a church (c.1215,2)

2. Hear presbyteral council and obtain consent of those with vested rights to convert a church to secular purposes for reasons other than irremediable disrepair (c.1222,2)

3. Visit proposed site of oratory personally or through another before permitting its erection (c.1224,1)

b. Sacred Times
Nothing explicit

III. The Bishop's Teaching Ministry

In the exercise of teaching authority by bishops, preaching the word takes the pride of place (*LG* 25; cf. *Directory on the Pastoral Ministry of Bishops*, par. 55). In addition to this kerygmatic witness of the bishop, there is a more formal teaching role which calls him to preserve and protect the truth of faith. This responsibility is commonly perceived as a defensive one, but it is understood more properly in a positive and productive way, namely as the transmission of the authentic gospel of Christ. The bishop teaches in this sense by reason of his position in the church over which he presides, in union with the head and other members of the episcopal college. He teaches in the name of the church and is authorized to make the final prudential judgment as to how the community's faith will be publicly expressed at various stages of its historical development. This can be done most appropriately only if the bishop is also accustomed to consult the faithful on matters of faith and Christian living . . . in his care for the unity and integrity of faith the bishop must respect the gift which the Holy Spirit imparts to members of the church for their witness to Christ. . . . In short the teaching responsibility of bishops is a specifically pastoral one, grounded in their role as leaders who serve the unity and growth of faith of the ecclesial community.
"In Service to the Gospel: A Consensus Statement of the Joint Committee" in *Cooperation between Theologians and the Ecclesiastical Magisterium*, L. O'Donovan, ed., p. 12

A. Rights of Bishops

1. Introductory Canons
1. Function as authentic doctor and teacher of faith (c.753)

2. Establish practical norms on ecumenical movement in light of the directives of supreme Church authority (c. 755,2)

2. Ministry of the Divine Word

a. *Preaching the Word of God*

1. Preach anywhere unless the local ordinary refuses authorization (c.763) (*ius*)
2. Restrict or remove preaching faculties for priest or deacon (c.764)
3. Issue norms on parish missions (c.770)
4. Determine norms on preaching in diocese (c.772,1)

b. *Catechetics*

1. Issue norms on catechetical activity in the diocese in light of Holy See norms (c.775,1)

3. Missionary Activity of the Church

Nothing explicit

4. Catholic Education

a. *Schools*

* 1. Approve schools to be established by religious (c.801)
2. Develop policies regarding Catholic religious education in diocese (c.804,1) (conference of bishops to publish general norms on such)
* 3. Name or approve religion teachers in his diocese and, if necessary for reasons of faith or morals, remove or require removal of a teacher (c.805) (*ius*)
* 4. Be vigilant over and visit Catholic schools in his diocese and develop policies regarding the general organization of such schools including those of religious with due regard for proper autonomy of latter in distinctly religious community matters (c.806,1) (*ius*)

b. *Catholic Universities and Institutes of Higher Learning*

1. Be vigilant over fidelity to Catholic principles in Catholic universities in diocese (c.810,2) (*ius*). Canon 810,1 provides that university statutes are to determine who is competent authority to hire professors and remove them according to procedures clarified in the same statutes.
2. Grant mandate to teach theological disciplines in

any institute of higher learning (c.812) ('competent authority' referred to in canon; hence perhaps not necessarily individual bishops)

c. Ecclesiastical Universities and Faculties

1. Vigilance role noted above in c.810,2 is applicable to ecclesiastical universities and faculties also (c.818).

2. Mandate-granting role noted above in c.812 is also applicable to ecclesiastical universities and faculties (c.818).

d. Media of Social Communications and Especially Books

* 1. Be vigilant lest faithful be harmed by publications/media as regards matters of faith or morals; require that writings of faith or morals be submitted to his judgment; repudiate works contrary to faith or morals (c.823) (*ius*) (reference also to particular councils and to conference of bishops in this area)

2. The 'local ordinary' for the approval of books is normally the local ordinary of the author or publisher (c.824,1: relevant to subsequent references in this section).

3. The local ordinary of the publisher is to approve the reprinting of liturgical books and translations and verify concordance with official edition; approve prayer books for public or private use of the faithful (c.826,2-3).

4. Approve catechisms and other resource materials for catechetical purposes (c.827,1)

5. Choose censor to assist in making judgment on permission to publish a given work (c.830,1) (*ius*) (possible help from list of censors drawn up by conference of bishops)

6. Approve work for publication or deny such approval giving reasons to the author (c.830,3)

7. Authorize clerics or religious to publish in journals generally contrary to faith and good morals (c.831,1)

B. Responsibilities of Bishops

1. Introductory Canons

1. Foster ecumenical movement (cc.755,2; 383,3)

2. Ministry of the Divine Word

1. Supervise exercise of ecclesial task of announcing the Gospel (c.756,2) (CC.757-759 speak of involvement of priests, deacons, religious and the rest of the Christian faithful in this evangelical enterprise. See also c.386,1)

2. Be solicitous for the pastoral care of those outside of mainstream of ecclesial life and provide for preaching of Gospel to nonbelievers (c.771) (See also c.383,1,4)

3. General catechetical responsibility vis-à-vis People of God (c.773) (reference generically to 'pastors of souls')

4. See to it that catechetical resources are available, prepare catechism if necessary, foster and coordinate catechetical undertakings (c.775,1)

5. Issue norms on various aspects of catechetics in light of which individual pastors function in their comparable ministry (c.777)

6. See to formation and continuing education of catechists (c.780)

3. Missionary Activity of the Church

1. Be solicitous about Church's missionary enterprise (c.782,2) (see also c.383,2)

4. Catholic Education

Introductory Canons

1. See to it that all the faithful may enjoy Catholic education (c.794,2)(reference generically to 'pastors of souls')

a. Schools

1. See to establishment of schools where education is imbued with a Christian spirit if such are lacking (c.802,1)

2. Supervise religious formation and education in schools and in communications media (c.804,1) (conference of bishops also competent in this area)

3. See to proper qualifications of those teaching religion in all types of schools (c.804,2)

4. Be vigilant that heads of Catholic schools fulfill responsibility to provide quality education (c.806,2)

b. Catholic Universities and Institutes of Higher Learning

1. Be vigilant over fidelity to Catholic principles in Catholic universities in diocese (c.810,2)

2. See to erection of theological faculty or at least a chair of theology in Catholic universities (c.811,1) (reference to 'competent authority' in canon)

* 3. Provide for pastoral care of college students even those in non-Catholic colleges (c.813)

c. Ecclesiastical Universities and Faculties

* 1. Provide for pastoral care of students in such universities and faculties (c.818 applying c.813 in this chapter)

* 2. Send talented students to ecclesiastical universities and faculties (c.819)

* 3. Establish institutes of higher religious studies where possible (c.821) (conference of bishops also responsible)

d. Media of Social Communications and Especially Books

1. Use modern media in fulfilling ministry of teaching and see to the education of the faithful in their correct use (c.822,1-2) (reference generically to 'pastors of Church')

* 2. Be vigilant lest faithful be harmed by publications/media as regards matters of faith or morals; require that writings on faith or morals be submitted to his judgment; repudiate works contrary to faith or morals (c.823) (reference also to particular councils and to conference of bishops in this area)

IV. The Bishop's Pastoral Government Ministry

A. The Bishop as Legislator in the Particular Church

The bishops, as vicars and legates of Christ, govern the particular churches assigned to them by their counsels, exhortations and example, but over and above that also by the authority and sacred power which indeed they exercise exclusively for the spiritual development of their flock in truth and holiness, keeping in mind that he who is the greater should become as the lesser and he who is the leader as the servant (cf.Lk.22:26-27). This power, which they exercise personally in the name of Christ, is proper, ordinary and immediate, although its exercise is ultimately controlled by the supreme authority of the Church and can be confined within certain limits should the usefulness of the Church and the faithful require that. In virtue of this power bishops have a sacred right and a duty before the Lord of legislating for and of passing judgment on their subjects, as well as of regulating everything that concerns the good order of divine worship and the apostolate.

Lumen gentium 27: Austin Flannery, OP, ed., *Vatican Council II, The Conciliar and Post Conciliar Documents*, pp. 382-383

1. Legislative Competence in the Particular Church

In law the bishop is the legislative authority for the portion of the People of God entrusted to his care (c.391); even when laws are passed in the collegial context of a diocesan synod, the bishop is technically the sole legislator (c.466). The bishop may not issue legislation contrary to laws passed by higher authority; if his legislation is contrary, it does not bind. Furthermore the bishop's legislative authority can be delegated only in those cases explicitly specified in law (c.135,2) (391,2); however, from a practical standpoint the bishop's reliance on various consultative organs to be discussed subsequently may be tantamount to delegating such legislative authority. This restrictiveness in law regarding the bishop's legislative authority is quite in contrast to the relatively broad options for his delegating judicial and executive authority or for his functioning through various vicars in different areas (c.391,2) (cc.475-481).

2. Those Subject to the Legislative Authority of the Bishop

(1) Catholics who have a domicile or quasi-domicile (c.102,1-2) in the diocese as long as they are actually present within it (c.12,3)

(2) Visitors in the diocese but only in the following matters:

  a) laws affecting public order;
  b) laws regulating the proper solemnities of acts;
  c) laws affecting permanent structures, e.g., sanctuaries (c.13,2,2⁰)

(3) Migrants or wanderers without their own proper domicile or quasi-domicile (c.13,3)

3. Possible Forms of Particular Legislation in a Diocese

(1) Synodal legislation (cc.460-468)
(2) General decrees (c.29)
(3) Authentic interpretation of a diocesan law by the bishop or one delegated by him (c.16,1-2)

Comparable to laws though not technically such are *general executory decrees* issued by one with executive authority. They are geared to clarifying in detail how the laws are to be applied and observed. An example might be detailed guidelines on premarital preparation to implement synodal legislation in this regard. Such general executory decrees are to be promulgated and have a *vacatio legis* (c.31).

Finally one should note briefly the binding force of *custom* even if *praeter ius* or *contra ius* (beyond the scope of the law or contrary to the law) after *30 years* even without the ratification of the bishop; the exception to this rule involves customs contrary to laws explicitly forbidding such customs; in this instance only a centenary or immemorial custom prevails with the force of law (c.26).

4. Possible Models of Exercising the Bishop's Legislative Function

a. The Executive Model: The Episcopal Council

A relatively limited form of consultation that a bishop might utilize in issuing diocesan legislation is the so-called *executive model* which has been used frequently in the past and involves selected administrators proposing rules and regulations in their particular areas to the bishop. He then in turn issues such norms in his own name as diocesan policy, e.g., in monitoring the exercise of financial administration in the diocese.

The revised Code provides for a so-called episcopal council to coordinate various pastoral activities; such a body is composed of the vicar(s) general and the episcopal vicar(s) (c.473,4). This may seem to be a fairly restricted group in light of the phenomenon of much more diversified clerical and lay participation in diocesan decision-making in various dioceses, yet there is no reason why the bishop may not establish a comparable body with much broader representation. The episcopal council itself is optional, presumably in light of the supreme legislator's reluctance to impede bishops in fashioning appropriate consultative mechanisms in light of diocesan needs and resources.

b. The Synodal Model: The Diocesan Synod

The bishop is technically the sole legislator in the diocese. However, the synod is envisioned as a potentially significant consultative body composed of selected priests and other Christian faithful, whose task is to assist the bishop in legislating for the particular church and the common pastoral good (c.460).

The following outline briefly indicates some key points on this institute in the revised Code:
(a) *Frequency*: time for holding of synod not specified

in law; it is to be determined by the bishop after consultation with the presbyteral council (c.461,1).

(b) *Authority in Synod*:

1) Diocesan bishop convokes, can suspend and dissolve (cc.462,1; 468,1).

2) Diocesan bishop presides personally or through vicar general or episcopal vicar as delegate (c.462,2).

3) Diocesan bishop is sole legislator (c.466).

4) Diocesan bishop is only one to sign decrees, and only on his authority are they made public (c.466).

5) Other members of synod have consultative vote after an open discussion of issues on the agenda (cc.465-466).

(c) *Members*:

1) Who *must* be invited (c.463,1):

    a. Coadjutor and auxiliary bishops

    b. Vicars general, episcopal, judicial

    c. Members of presbyteral council

    d. Lay Christians including religious, designated by diocesan pastoral council according to a method and in a number determined by the bishop; if there is no diocesan pastoral council, the bishop determines the way laity are represented.

    e. Rectors of major seminary

    f. Deans

    g. Presbyter and alternate from each deanery elected by all exercising pastoral ministry in deanery

    h. Superiors of religious institutes in diocese

2) Who *may* be invited (c.463,2-3)

    a. Other clergy, religious, laypersons (c.463,2)

    b. Non-Catholic observers (c.463,3)

(d) *Other pertinent norms*:

1) Synodal decrees are to be communicated by the bishop to the metropolitan and the conference of bishops (c.467).

2) In a *sede vacante*, or *sede impedita* situation the synod is suspended *ipso iure*; the new bishop must dissolve or continue it (c.468,2).

c. The Conciliar Model: The Presbyteral and Pastoral Councils

On a somewhat smaller scale than the diocesan synod, the mandatory presbyteral council and the optional diocesan pastoral council offer another possible model of corporate ecclesial involvement in the bishop's legislative function. In this connection some brief comments on the college of consultors are also warranted.

The Presbyteral Council (cc.495-501)

1. *Notion*: A mandatory body of priests who are to be a kind of senate of the bishop, representing the entire presbyterate; this council is to aid the bishop in the government of the diocese according to the norm of law, in order that the pastoral welfare of the portion of the people of God committed to him may be carried forward as effectively as possible (c.495,1).

2. *Statutes*: The council is to have its own statutes approved by the diocesan bishop; they are to take into account the Code and possible norms of the conference of bishops among other things (c.496).

3. *Principle for electing members*: The presbyterate is to be duly represented, especially in light of the diversity of ministries and regions of the diocese; this is to be determined by the statutes (c.499).

4. *Membership* (c.497):
   1) About half are to be elected by the priests of the diocese
   2) There are to be some *ex officio* members as determined by the statutes
   3) The diocesan bishop can freely name other members

5. *Active and passive voice* (c.498):
   1) By right
      a. All secular priests incardinated in the diocese
      b. Other priests not incardinated but resident and exercising some office for the good of the diocese
   2) By extension: other priests who have a domicile or a quasi-domicile in the diocese to the extent that the statutes provide for this

6. *Role of the bishop:*

1) To convoke and preside over the council though the actual calling of meetings and chairing the sessions could be done by someone else (c.500,1)

2) To determine the questions to be treated and receive proposals from members though this does not preclude other priests in the diocese from submitting items for the agenda (c.500,1)

3) To publicize what was determined at council meetings (c.500,3)

7. *Required consultation*: The bishop is to consult the council in significant issues in general and specifically in making decisions in the following areas:

1) The advisability of a diocesan synod (c.461,1)

2) The modification of parishes, e.g., their erection, modification, division or suppression (c.515,2)

3) The determination of the use of offerings of the faithful made on the occasion of parish services and placed in a general parish fund (c.531)

4) The appropriateness of parish councils (c.536,1)

5) The granting of permission to build a church (c.1215,2)

6) The granting of permission for a church to be converted to secular purposes for reasons other than its poor condition (c.1222,2)

7) The imposition of a tax for the needs of the diocese on public juridic persons subject to the bishop; also the imposition of an extraordinary and moderate tax for very grave needs on other juridic persons and on physical persons (c.1263)

8. *Cessation*

1) *Sede vacante* (when the see is vacant); yet new bishop is to reconstitute it within a year (c.501,2)

2) Bishop may dissolve the council if it gravely abuses its function after consulting the metropolitan; yet it is to be reconstituted within a year; if the metropolitan wishes to dissolve the council, he is to consult the suffragan who is senior in terms of promotion (c.501,3).

The College of Consultors (c.502)

1. *Notion*: a group of between six to 12 priests cho-

sen by the bishop for a five-year term from among the members of the presbyteral council to exercise various functions prescribed by law

   2. *Functions*:

      1) When the see is filled:

The bishop is to obtain the *consent* of the college to:

a. Perform acts of extraordinary administration (c.1277)

b. Alienate diocesan property (c.1292,1)

c. Authorize alienation within minimal and maximal sums set by the conference of bishops in case of juridic persons subject to bishop (c.1293,1)

d. The bishop is to *consult* the college in the appointment and removal of the diocesan finance officer (c.494,1-2).

      2) When the see is impeded: the college is to elect an administrator if no other provision has been made (c.413,2).

      3) When the see is vacant:

a. The administrator must obtain the *consent* of the college of consultors for the incardination, excardination or emigration of clerics after the see is vacant for a year (c.272) and for the removal of the chancellor or other notaries (c.485).

b. The college of consultors fulfills the role of the presbyteral council (c.501,2).

c. If there is no auxiliary bishop, the college of consultors governs the diocese initially provided no other arrangement has been made by the Holy See (c.419).

d. The college of consultors is to elect an administrator within eight days of the vacancy of the see (c.421,1).

e. The college of consultors is to notify the Holy See of the vacancy if there is no auxiliary bishop (c.422).

The Diocesan Pastoral Council (cc.511-514)

   1. *Notion and establishment*: In each diocese, to the extent that pastoral circumstances recommend it, a pastoral council is to be constituted whose responsi-

bility is to investigate under the authority of the bishop all those things which pertain to pastoral works, to ponder them, and to propose practical conclusions about them (c.511).

2. *Status*: to be established where pastoral circumstances recommend it (c.511); to be constituted for a definite period of time (c.513,1); to be called together at least once a year (c.514,2) and to cease functioning when the see is vacant (c.513,2)

3. *Membership*: clerics, religious and especially laity representative of the diversity of the diocese in terms of regions, social conditions, professions and activity in the apostolate (c.512)

4. *Role*: strictly consultative in terms of examining pastoral activities and the needs of the apostolate yet not being engaged in diocesan government in the strict sense (cc.511; 514)

5. *Role of the bishop*:

1. To convoke and preside over the council though the actual calling of meetings and chairing the sessions could be done by someone else (c.514,1)

2. To issue statutes for the council (c.513,1)

3. To determine norms for the selection of council members (c.512,1)

5. Possible Areas for Diocesan Legislation

1) References to *diocesan bishop's* initiative explicitly:

1. Supervision of clerical behavior in relationship to persons who might jeopardize celibate commitment (c.277,3)

2. Approval of statutes of presbyteral council (c.496)

3. Formulation of statutes of diocesan pastoral council (c.513,1)

4. Use of parish offerings ('stole fees') contained in parish fund (c.531); presbyteral council to be consulted

5. Provision for pastoral care when pastor is absent (c.533,3)

6. Development of supplementary parish registers (c.535,1) (conference of bishops also competent)

7. Norms for parish pastoral councils (c.536,1)

8. Norms for parish finance boards (c.537)

9. Norms on parish missions (c.770)

10. Supplementary norms on preaching in diocese (c.772,1)

11. Norms on catechetics in diocese (c.775,1)

12. Norms on sacramental preparation and other parish educational tasks (c.777)

13. Norms on Catholic religious education and formation (c.804,1) (conference of bishops also competent)

14. Norms on sacramental sharing (c.844,5): consultation with hierarchs of other communions (conference of bishops also other competent)

15. Norms on activity of extraordinary minister of exposition and reposition (c.943)

16. Norms on situations warranting general absolution in light of criteria agreed upon with the other bishops if general guidelines are to be drawn up (c.961,2)

17. Norms on communal anointing services (c.1002)

18. Norms on liturgy of the word in situations where normal Eucharistic participation is impossible (c.1248,2)

19. Determine meaning of acts of extraordinary administration if it is not specified in the statutes of a juridic person (c.1277)

2) Explicit references to local ordinary or ordinary:

1. Use of stipends above and beyond one permitted celebrant per day ordinarily (c.951,1) This refers to proper ordinary of celebrant not local ordinary where Mass is celebrated unless it is a matter of pastors or parochial vicars.

2. Organization of premarital preparation (c. 1064)

3. Approval of marriage of certain members of faithful because of certain pastoral concerns (c.1071)

4. Approval of statutes of diocesan shrine (c.1232,1)

3) Explicit reference to particular law:

1. Continuing education of the clergy (c.279,2)

2. Specification of residence obligation and vacation time for clergy (universal law determination also relevant) (c.283)

3. Clarification of activities inappropriate for clerics (c.285,1)

4. Faculties for deans (c.555,1) (universal law determinations also here)

5. Faculties for preaching (c.764)

6. Norms on Christian burial (c.1243)

7. Norms on conditions for accepting pious foundations (c.1304,2) (universal law determinations also here)

8. Norms on formalities of expediting citations and other comparable judicial acts (c.1509,1)

B. The Bishop as Administrator

1. General Principles on Administrative Activity

Since a significant part of episcopal legal ministry involves the issuance of various administrative decrees, the highlighting of some particularly noteworthy canons in this respect may be helpful.

1. *Notion* of administrative decree: an act issued by a competent executive authority in which a decision is given or a provision is made in a particular case in accord with the norms of law (c.48). General norms also valid for individual precept whereby a person is directly and legitimately enjoined to do or omit something especially in view of enforcing the law (c.49).

2. *Data-gathering and consultation* (c.50):

   a) Before issuing a decree an administrator is to seek out the information and proofs necessary for such a decision.

   b) Furthermore, to the extent that it is possible, the administrator is to hear those whose rights could be violated by a given decision.

3. Issuing of *decision in writing* (c.51): an administrative decree is to be issued in writing with at least a summary exposition of the reasons prompting it although for the most serious of reasons a copy of it need not necessarily be given to the party for whom it is intended; yet the decree should be communicated orally to such a party (c.55).

4. *Time-limit for issuing decree* (c.57): if the law requires the issuance of a decree or an interested party presents a legitimate petition or recourse, an administrator is to ac-

knowledge such and provide accordingly in three months unless the law provides for a different time limit; should no decree be issued, a negative response is presumed; yet the decree is still to be issued and any damages are to be compensated for.

5. *Interpretation* of decree (c.36):

a) *Basic principle*: decrees are to be interpreted in accordance with the proper meaning of the words and common usage.

b) In doubt a decree is to be broadly interpreted unless it:

1) refers to lawsuits;

2) involves threatening or inflicting of penalties;

3) restricts the rights of persons;

4) injures vested rights;

5) is opposed to the law for the convenience of private individuals.

6. *Validity* of decree: two points to be kept in mind are the following: a decree is invalid if it injures the vested right of another or is contrary to the law or an approved custom unless the competent authority adds a clause expressly derogating from the law (c.38).

2. The Bishop's Involvement in Various Personnel Issues

a. *Relationship to Coadjutor and Auxiliary Bishops*

The coadjutor and the auxiliary bishop are viewed as key collaborators with the diocesan bishop in various aspects of diocesan government, especially in the administrative arena. They are not treated with other significant officials of the diocesan curia in the revised Code but rather in a separate section given their status in the particular church (cc.403-411). Hence it seems appropriate to discuss their role briefly here prior to considering the diocesan bishop's responsibilities and prerogatives in choosing significant leadership personnel at the diocesan, parish and deanery level.

1) Appointment

1) Initiative of the diocesan bishop in requesting *auxiliary* bishop because of pastoral needs of diocese (c.403,1)

2) Initiative from other sources, e.g., Holy See in naming *auxiliary with special faculties* for more serious reasons even of a personal nature or a *coadjutor bishop* who enjoys special faculties and the right of succession (c.403,2-3)

2) Taking possession of office

1) Coadjutor presents letter of appointment to bishop and college of consultors in presence of chancellor who records such (c.404,1).

2) Auxiliary presents letter of appointment to bishop in presence of chancellor who records such (c.404,2).

3) If diocesan bishop is incapacitated, it suffices for both the coadjutor and the auxiliary to present their letters to the college of consultors in the presence of the chancellor who records such (c.404,3).

3) Status of coadjutor and auxiliary

a) When the see is occupied:

1) To be determined from canons of revised Code and letter of appointment (c.405,1).

2) To aid diocesan bishop in diocesan government and take his place if he is absent or impeded (c.405,2).

3) To be named vicar general and to receive the special mandate for various administrative tasks in preference to all others if one is named coadjutor or an auxiliary with special faculties (c.406,1).

4) To be named vicar general or at least episcopal vicar while being dependent on the bishop alone or on the coadjutor and special auxiliary mentioned above if one is named a simple auxiliary (c.406,2).

5) To be consulted by the diocesan bishop on matters of pastoral importance in preference to others and to work harmoniously with the diocesan bishop and with one another (c.407).

6) To fulfill diocesan functions as requested by the diocesan bishop who is not to commit to others episcopal rights and functions which the coadjutor or auxiliary is capable of performing (c.408).

b) When the see is vacant:

1) Coadjutor becomes bishop of diocese if he has taken legitimate possession (c.409,1).

2) Auxiliaries retain the power they possessed as vicar general or episcopal vicar while the see was filled; and they exercise them under the authority of the apostolic/diocesan administrator if they are not designated as such; this rule presupposes that no other arrangements are made by the competent authority (c.409,2).

b. Relationship to Other Significant Leadership Personnel at Various Levels

Canon 157, a general canon on ecclesiastical offices reads as follows:

Unless something else is explicitly stated in law, it is the responsibility of the diocesan bishop to provide for ecclesiastical offices in his own particular church.

The following reflections take the above principle as a point of departure and highlight the various dimensions of episcopal rights and responsibilities regarding appointment to various offices at the diocesan, parish and deanery level.

Rather than discuss these issues in two separate sections under the headings "rights of bishops" and "responsibilities of bishops," it seems more appropriate here to treat the various concerns in a somewhat more integral fashion. The order of the canons will be followed, and the key points highlighted in them will be summarized.

1) **Diocesan Curia:** institutions and persons assisting bishop in the government of the whole diocese, i.e., in directing pastoral activity, administering the diocese and exercising judicial power (c.469)

   a) *General Rules*

   a) Bishop competent to name all members of the curia (c.470)

   b) Curia members to take oath of office to serve faithfully and maintain secrecy where demanded by law or bishop (c.471)

b) Specific Offices in the Administrative Arena

(1) Moderator of Curia (or Chief Executive Officer)

a) *Description of office*: coordinates administrative activities of diocese under the authority of the bishop and ensures faithful fulfillment of office by other members of curia (c.473,2).

b) *Appointment*: optional (c.473,2)

c) *Qualifications*: priest (c.473,2) and preferably but not necessarily vicar general or one of the vicars general (c.473,3)

(2) Vicar General

a) *Description of office*: possesses ordinary executive power comparable to bishop throughout diocese except for those matters bishop reserves to himself or those areas where law requires a *special mandate* (generally speaking all parts of this manual where an asterisk precedes description of a given episcopal right or responsibility) (cc.475,1; 479,1).

b) *Appointment*: obligatory (c.475,1): generally one unless size of diocese, number of faithful or other pastoral reasons suggest otherwise (c.475,2)

c) *Qualifications*: priest, at least 30 years of age, S.T.D./S.T.L. or J.C.D./J.C.L. or at least expert in theology or canon law, orthodox, good character, prudent and experienced in administration: not canon penitentiary or related to the bishop closer than fourth degree (c.478)

d) *Duration of office*: at the disposition of the bishop who freely names and removes from office unless vicar general is a bishop (c.477,1)

e) *Loss of office*: removal as above, expiration of mandate, resignation or *sede vacante* unless vicar general is a bishop (cc.481,1; 409,2)

(3) Episcopal Vicar

a) *Description of office*: possesses ordinary executive power comparable to bishop for his particular sphere of competence (certain geographical area, certain type of ministry, particular rite, etc.) except for those matters the bishop reserves to himself or those areas where law requires a *special mandate* (generally speaking all parts of this manual where an asterisk precedes description of a given episcopal right or responsibility) (cc.476; 479,1).

b) *Appointment*: *optional* depending on diocesan needs; one or several as necessary (c.476)

c) *Qualifications*: priest, at least 30 years of age, S.T.D./S.T.L. or J.C.D./J.C.L. or at least expert in theology or canon law, orthodox, good character, prudent and experienced in administration, not canon penitentiary or related to the bishop closer than four degrees (c.478)

d) *Duration of office*: at the disposition of the bishop who freely names and removes from office; yet generally to be appointed for a term of office unlike vicar general unless episcopal vicar is a bishop (c.477,1)

e) *Loss of office*: removal as above, expiration of mandate, resignation or *sede vacante* unless episcopal vicar is a bishop (cc.481,1; 409,2)

(4) Chancellor

a) *Description of office*: sees to it that curial acts are drawn up and expedited and that they are safeguarded in the archives (c.482,1).

b) *Appointment*: *obligatory* (c.482,1); additional vice-chancellors are optional

c) *Qualifications*: cleric or layperson; good character and above reproach; priest necessary only in cases in which the reputa-

tion of a priest could be jeopardized
(c.483,2)

d) *Duration of office*: at the disposition of
the bishop who freely may remove chancellor from office (c.485) (diocesan administrator needs *consent* of college of consultors to do so)

(5) **Notary**

a) *Description of office*: authenticates all
curial acts, only judicial acts or acts in a
particular case (c.483,1).

b) *Appointment*: *optional* above and beyond chancellor, who is viewed as pri-
mary notary (c.483, 1)

c) *Qualifications*: clerk or layperson; good
character and above reproach; priest necessary only in cases in which the reputation of a priest could be jeopardized
(c.483,2)

d) *Duration of office*: at the disposition of
the bishop who freely may remove notary from office (c.485) (diocesan administrator needs *consent* of college of consultors to do so)

(6) **Finance Council**

a) *Description of office*: approves annual financial statement of diocese and pre-
pares annual budget in accordance with
directions of the bishop; to be consulted
or to give approval to bishop for various
administrative decisions of a financial
character, especially but not exclusively
specified in Book V on the Church's temporal goods (c.493).

Bishop to *consult* finance council in
following matters:

a. Appointment and removal of fiscal
officer (c.494,1-2)

b. Imposing of taxes on physical and
juridical persons (c.1263)

c. Positing of significant administrative acts in light of the economic condition of the diocese (c.1277)

d. Determining the meaning of acts of extraordinary administration for institutes subject to his control if the statutes do not specify this (c.1281,2)

e. Authorizing the placing of money and mobile goods in a safe place and investing them (c.1305)

f. Reducing of burdens imposed in executing last wills for pious causes if such burdens cannot be fulfilled (c.1310,2)

Bishop to obtain *consent* of finance council in following matters:

a. Positing acts of extraordinary administration (c.1277)

b. Authorizing alienation of Church goods within minimal and maximal sums determined by conference of bishops in case of juridic persons subject to him (c.1292,1)

c. Alienating diocesan property (c.1292,1)

b) *Appointment*: *obligatory* (c.492,1); council presided over by bishop or delegate

c) *Qualifications*: at least three of the faithful to be named; clerics or laypersons skilled in financial matters and civil law; outstanding in character; not related to the bishop closer than fourth degree (c.492,1,3)

d) *Duration of office*: to be named for a five-year term, which may be renewed for other quinquennia (c.492,2)

(7) **Fiscal Officer**

a) *Description of office*: administers temporal goods of diocese under authority of bishop and in accord with budget determined by finance council, pays diocesan bills and makes annual financial report among other things (c.494,3-4).

b) *Appointment*: *obligatory* after consultation by bishop with college of consultors and finance council (c.494,1)

c) *Qualifications*: cleric or layperson, expert in financial affairs, of high integrity (c.494,1)

d) *Duration of office*: to be named for a five-year term, which may be renewed for other quinquennia; removal for serious reason by the bishop after consulting the college of consultors and finance council (c.494,2)

c) Specific Offices in the Judicial Arena

(1) Officialis or Vicar Judicial

a) *Description of office*: possesses ordinary judicial power comparable to bishop with whom he constitutes one tribunal; he judges all cases except those the bishop reserves to himself or law reserves to others (c.1420,1-2).

b) *Appointment*: obligatory (c.1420,1); adjunct or vice-officialis *facultative*

c) *Qualifications*: Priest, good character, J.C.L. or J.C.D., at least 30 years of age (c.1420,4); different person from vicar general unless small size of diocese or not too burdensome court docket suggests otherwise (c.1420,1)

d) *Duration of office*: to be named for definite term of office and not to be removed from office by the bishop except for legitimate and serious reason (c.1422); does not cease from office *sede vacante* and may not be removed by diocesan administrator; needs reconfirmation by the new bishop (c.1420,5).

(2) Judge

a) *Description of office*: assists vicar judicial or officialis in judging nonreserved cases

b)*Appointment*: obligatory (c.1421,1)

c) *Qualifications*: clerics as a rule (c.1421,1) (priests or deacons); laypersons, men or women, if necessary may function with two or more clerics on a collegiate tribunal if authorized by conference of bishops (c.1421,2); of good character and J.C.D. or J.C.L. (c.1421,3)

d) *Duration of office*: to be named for a definite term and removable by the bishop only for a legitimate and grave cause (c.1422)

(3) Auditor

a) *Description of office*: assists tribunal in various ways prescinding from rendering definitive decision, e.g., gathering proofs and forwarding them to judge (c.1428,3).

b) *Appointment*: *optional* on part of the judge or president of collegiate tribunal (c.1428,1)

c) *Qualifications*: cleric or layperson who is a diocesan judge or another person approved by the bishop; good character, prudent and knowledgeable (c.1428,1-2)

(4) Promotor of Justice

a) *Description of office*: provides for the interests of the common good in contentious cases in which public good is at stake as well as in criminal cases (c.1430).

b) *Appointment*: *mandatory* in cases when the bishop judges public good to be at stake or when the law requires such or when the nature of the matter calls for such intervention (cc.1430; 1431,1); appointment for all such cases or for individual cases (c.1436,2)

c) *Qualifications*: cleric or layperson, man or woman, of good character, J.C.D. or J.C.L., prudent, zealous for justice (c.1435)

d) *Duration of office*: removable for just cause by bishop (c.1436,2)

(5) Defender of Bond

a) *Description of office*: proposes whatever can be reasonably articulated contrary to nullity or dissolution of marriage or nullity of ordination (c.1432).

45

b) *Appointment*: *mandatory* in above-mentioned cases (c.1432); appointment for all such cases or for a single case (c.1432,2)

c) *Qualifications*: cleric or layperson, man or woman, of good character, J.C.D. or J.C.L., prudent, zealous for justice (c.1435)

d) *Duration of office*: removable for just cause by bishop (c.1436,2)

(6) Advocate

a) *Description of office*: aids petitioner or respondent throughout process through legal expertise.

b) *Appointment:* *optional* in marriage cases (c.1481,1,3) at initiative of petitioner or respondent (in nonconsummation cases not advocate technically but jurisprudent may be named by bishop—c.1701,2) c.1701,2)

c) *Qualifications*: canonically an adult (18 years of age), good reputation, Catholic unless the bishop approves a non-Catholic, J.C.D. or otherwise expert and approved by bishop; need to receive authentic mandate to be left at tribunal (c.1483; 1484,1)

d) *Duration of office*: possible removal by one constituting him or her (c.1486,1); possible rejection by judge *ex officio* or at the request of the party for a grave reason (c.1487); possible suspension from office or removal from approved roster of advocates by bishop (c.1488)

2) Parish Level

a) *Pastors*

1. *Description of office (briefly)*: exercises leadership role in the parish entrusted to him under the authority of the diocesan bishop, in whose ministry he is called to share, fulfilling the ministries of teaching, sanctifying and governing with the cooperation of other priests, deacons and the laity according to law (cc.519; 515,1).

2. *Appointment*: *obligatory* for officially constituted parish (c.515,1) although at times
pastoral care for other types of communities
can be provided for in other ways (c.516,2)
and at times a participation in the pastoral
care of a parish/quasi-parish can be entrusted
to one who is not a priest or to a group who
are not priests under the pastoral supervision
of a priest however (c.517,2)

3. *Qualifications*: for validity a priest
(c.521,1); for liceity one who is outstanding
in doctrine and moral character, pastorally
zealous and characterized by those qualities
appropriate for pastoral leadership in universal or particular law (c.821,2); suitability to be
certain in the judgment of the bishop, even
through exam if necessary (c.521,3)

4. *Consultation* before appointment by the bishop
with dean, if such exists (mandatory) and certain
priests and laity if necessary (optional) (c.524) (no
explicit reference to personnel board as such in revised law; yet it might appropriately be consid-
ered in this context).

5. *Duration of office*: pastor to be appointed for an
indefinite time for the sake of pastoral stability
yet the bishop may possibly appoint for term of
office if approved by conference of bishops
(c.522) whose decree is to be confirmed by the
Holy See. In the United States appointment is for
six years with possible renewal.

6. *Obligation of residence*: in principle the pastor
is to reside in a parish house near the church;
however, in individual cases the local ordinary
may permit the former to reside elsewhere, especially but not exclusively in a common residence
for clerics as long as the pastoral ministry is not
thereby jeopardized (c.533,1).

7. *Loss of office* (c.538):
Expiration of term in accord with no. 5 above
Retirement: not required but encouraged at
age 75 (c.538,3); bishop to provide appropriate support and lodging.
Removal
   a) *General principle*: no one appointed to

an office for an indefinite period of time can be removed except for serious reasons and following the procedure described in law (c.193,1); no one appointed to an office for a definite term can be removed before the end of that term except for serious reasons and following the procedure described in law (c.193,2); applicability of this norm to pastors in c.1740.

b) *Specifics on removal of pastor:*

1. Causes for removal (c.1741)

Conditions which justify the removal of a pastor include behavior which may cause serious harm or disturbance to the ecclesial community; mental incompetence or permanent physical illness which renders the pastor incapable of carrying out his duties; loss of reputation in the eyes of serious-minded parishioners or hostility toward the pastor which is unlikely to dissipate soon; serious neglect or violation of pastoral responsibilities which persists in spite of warning; inefficient administration of temporal goods resulting in serious harm to the Church—a problem that can be dealt with only through removal of the pastor.

2. Procedure for removal (cc.1742-1747)

1) When the bishop has reason to believe there is sufficient cause for removal, he must confer with two pastors selected from among those approved for this purpose by the presbyteral council after being proposed by the bishop (c.1742,1) (formerly synodal examiners).

2) If after consultation with the two pastors the bishop feels that the serious reasons require the removal of the pastor, he will prudently ask the pastor to resign within 15 days. He is to indicate the reason(s) and arguments for removal for the validity of this invitation (c.1742,1).

3) If after two requests the pastor does not submit his resignation or refuses to do so without giving reasons, the bishop is to issue a decree of removal (c.1744,2).

4) If the pastor decides to contest the bishop's action, he is permitted to examine the records of the case and respond in writing. After examining the pastor's written response and, if necessary, after a hearing, the bishop is to discuss the matter with the same two pastors. After this deliberation, the bishop is to decide whether to remove him or not (c.1745).

5) Once the decree of removal has been issued, the pastor must vacate the parish. If the pastor is ill, the bishop should allow him to remain on the premises as long as necessary (c.1747,1-2).

6) The bishop must still provide for the sustenance of the pastor by giving him another assignment or by directly providing an adequate pension (c.1746).

7) The pastor still has recourse to the Congregation for Clergy against the bishop's decision.

8) During this recourse the bishop may not appoint another pastor but may appoint an administrator (c.1747,3).

N.B. As regards *religious pastors* cf.c.682,2 (removal at the will of either the bishop or religious superior, having informed the other but without needing the consent of the other).

Transfer

a) *General principle*: no one may be transferred unwillingly from an office unless there is a serious reason, and there is an opportunity to explain the reasons for one's unwillingness to be transferred and the procedures in law are followed (c.190,2); application to pastors (c.1748).

b) *Specifics on transfer of pastor*:

1. *Causes* for transfer (c.1748): good of persons and necessity or utility of the Church

2. *Procedure* for transfer (cc.1748-1752)

1) Bishop proposes the transfer in writing (c.1748).

2) If pastor refuses, he should give his reasons in writing (c.1749).

3) If the bishop's decision remains firm, he should follow the same procedure as that outlined for the removal of a pastor (cc.1750-1752).

b) *Team Ministry*

1. *Description of office*: instead of one priest functioning as pastor, the pastoral care of a parish or several parishes is entrusted to several priests acting as a team (c.517,1).

2. *Appointment*: *optional* depending on pastoral circumstances (c.517,1)

3. Above-mentioned rules for ordinary pastors in section 1) are in effect; however, in team ministry one priest is to function as *moderator* to coordinate the pastoral activity of the team and to respond to the bishop regarding its ministerial activities (c.517,1) as well as to represent the parish in legal matters (cc.543,2,3^0; 532).

4. Cessation from office by one member of the team does not mean that the parish is vacant; rather the bishop is to provide for the appointment of another member if appropriate and certainly for a moderator if he ceases from office for one reason or another; until appointment of a new moderator, senior member of team functions as such (c.544).

c) *Parochial Administrator*

1. *Description of office*: takes over interim leadership of parish during a vacancy for one reason or another or takes place of incapacitated pastor (c.539).

2. *Appointment*: *obligatory* by bishop in circumstances mentioned in no. 1.

3. *Qualifications*: priest for validity (c.539)

4. *Distinctive responsibilities* above and beyond basic rights and responsibilities of pas-

tors; do nothing that would be prejudicial to the rights of the pastor or the good of the parish; make report to pastor regarding stewardship when task is finished (c.540).

d) Parochial Vicar or Associate Pastor (Assistant/Curate)

1. *Description of office*: aids pastor and participates in his pastoral care with common deliberation and planning either in the whole of the parish ministry or in a certain part of the parish or for a certain group of the faithful or possibly fulfills specialized ministry in various parishes (c.545).

2. *Appointment: optional* depending on pastoral circumstances (c.545)

3. *Qualifications*: priest for validity (c.546)

4. *Consultation* by bishop prior to appointment optional with pastor(s) involved or dean (c.547)

5. *Duration of office*: at the disposition of the bishop who may freely remove as he has freely appointed; removal for a just cause yet no particular procedure required (cc.552; 193,3)

6. Obligation of *residence*: in principle the parochial vicar is to reside in the parish; yet the local ordinary may permit him to live elsewhere, especially but not exclusively in a common residence for clerics as long as the pastoral ministry is not thereby jeopardized (c.550,1); some kind of sharing of life between pastor and parochial vicars is encouraged where possible (c.550,2).

3) Deanery Level (cc.553-555)

a) *Description of office*: promotes and coordinates pastoral activities in the deanery in various ways specified in the revised Code (c.555) and in particular law.

b) *Appointment: obligatory* if deanery itself has been established in diocese; the former structure itself is facultative or optional (c.374,2) in contrast to the parish which is obligatory.

c) *Qualifications*: priest judged by bishop to be

suitable in light of circumstances of place and time; not necessarily to be pastor of a given parish (c.554,1)

d) *Consultation* with priests of deanery prior to appointment optional on part of bishop (c.553,2)

e) *Duration of office*: to be appointed for a definite term to be specified in particular law (c.554,2); removable by bishop for just cause (c.554,3)

C. The Bishop as Administrator Especially regarding the Stewardship of Temporalities

Because of his position as head of a particular church the bishop sees that he is serving charity and ecclesial fellowship by assuming his responsibility for the care and supervision of the administration of temporalities which are ordered to the divine worship, the charity and the apostolate of the church.

Therefore, following the instruction of the Holy See and the episcopal conferences he himself tries to manage the resource of the diocese . . . in such a way that charity is the first principle, the supreme law, and, as it were, the soul of his administration (cf. GS 25-31; 43; 63-72; AA 7; 13-14; 32).

After justice is assured, the following are the most salient features of this administration:

a) the pastoral principle which subordinates everything to the interest of piety, charity and the apostolate;

b) the cooperative principle which gives the diocese and parishes a share in the administration; for it should be the common action and common concern of the bishop along with the clergy and representatives of the faithful . . .;

c) the ascetical principle which, according to the spirit of the evangelical law (cf. Mt.19:21), demands that the disciples of Christ deal with the world as though they had no dealings with it (cf. 1 Cor.7:31): thus they are to be modest, free and unimpeded, trusting in divine Providence and open-handed to the needy, keeping the bond of charity (1 Jn. 3:17-18);

d) the principle of the good of the family in the work of administration.

Sacred Congregation for Bishops, *Directory on the Pastoral Ministry of Bishops*, 134

1. Rights of Bishops

a. *Acquisition of Goods*

* 1. Moderately tax for diocesan needs public juridic persons subject to him in a fashion proportionate to their income; in case of grave necessity impose a

moderate and extraordinary tax on physical persons and juridic persons not subject to him; proper consultation required (c.1263) (*ius*).

2. Authorize private physical or juridic persons to engage in fund raising (c.1265,1) (possible guidelines of conference of bishops on this: c.1265,2).

3. Prescribe special collection to be taken up in all churches for various ecclesial undertakings (c.1266).

4. Permit administrators to refuse gifts of some significance as well as to accept restricted gifts (c.1267,2).

b. Administration of Goods

1. Issue appropriate instructions on administration of goods of public juridic persons subject to him (c.1276,2).

2. Entrust various responsibilities to fiscal officer besides the following ones specified in law: administer the goods of the diocese under the authority of the bishop according to the policy established by the finance council; meet expenses which the bishop or others legitimately deputed have authorized (c.494,3). Among those responsibilities are those related to the bishop's vigilance over the administration of the goods of those juridic persons subject to him (c.1276) and to his naming administrators for juridic persons who don't have them (c.1279,2).

3. Intervene in case of administrative negligence (c.1279,1) (*ius*).

4. Name administrators for public juridic persons who do not have them (c.1279,2).

5. Permit administrators to posit acts of so-called extraordinary administration; determine such acts if not specified in statutes (c.1281,1-2).

6. Approve administrators investing excess capital (c.1284,2,6°).

7. Receive annual report from nonexempt administrators (c.1287,1).

8. Approve in writing administrators engaging in civil litigation (c.1288).

c. Contracts Especially Alienation

1. Authorize alienation of goods in case of juridic persons subject to him if value of goods within minimal and maximal sums determined by the confer-

ence of bishops; alienate goods of diocese; in both cases formalities of law to be followed (c.1292,1).

d. Pious Wills in General and Pious Foundations

1. As executor of pious wills, be vigilant over their fulfillment even through visitation if necessary; clauses contrary to such a right are viewed as not appended (c.1301) (*ius*).

2. Receive report of trustee(s) on stewardship of goods for pious causes; insist on safeguarding goods of trust (c.1302,1-2).

3. Approve in writing acceptance of foundation by a juridic person (c.1304,1).

4. Approve placing of money and mobile goods (dowry) in a safe place and investing such resources after due consultation (c.1305).

5. Reduce Mass obligations because of diminished revenue if provided for in rules of foundation (c.1308,2); reduce Masses provided for in wills (*Missas legatorum*) to diocesan stipend scale under certain circumstances (c.1308,3); reduce Mass burdens on ecclesiastical institutions if income insufficient for purposes of institution (c.1308,4). The competent authority in c.1308,2 is any ordinary; the competent authority in the other parts of the canon is the diocesan bishop.

6. Transfer Mass obligations to days, altars, or churches other than those specified in the statutes of the foundation; same authorities as in prior canon (c.1309).

7. Reduce, moderate or commute wills of faithful regarding a pious cause if such a power has been expressly granted by the author of the foundation (c.1310,1).

8. Reduce burdens (from wills) equitably if they cannot be fulfilled because of diminished revenue or some other cause through no fault on the part of the administrator(s); this requires consultation and does not apply to Mass obligations (c.1310,2).

2. Responsibilities of Bishops

a. Acquisition of Goods

1. Remind faithful of their obligation to support the church (c.1261,2).

* 2. Consult finance council and presbyteral council regarding imposition of a moderate tax for diocesan needs on public juridic persons subject to bishop and moderate extraordinary tax on physical persons and other juridic persons (c.1263).

3. Support Holy See in its service of the universal Church (c.1271).

b. Administration of Goods

* 1. Set up special fund for clergy support (c.281) if not otherwise provided for (c.1274,1); establish a common fund in diocese for support of other personnel and various ecclesial needs (c.1274,3).

2. Be vigilant over administration of goods of public juridic persons subject to him; issue appropriate instructions in fulfilling administrative oversight role (c.1276).

* 3. Consult finance council and college of consultors in positing significant administrative acts in light of economic condition of diocese (c.1277).

* 4. Obtain consent of finance council and college of consultors for acts of extraordinary administration (c.1277).

5. Submit annual report of nonexempt administrators to finance council for its examination (c.1287,1).

c. Contracts Especially Alienation

* 1. Obtain consent of finance council, interested parties and college of consultors to:
    a) authorize alienation of goods of juridic persons subject to him if their value falls within the minimal and maximal sums determined by the conference of bishops;
    b) alienate the goods of the diocese (c.1292,1).

d. Pious Wills in General and Pious Foundations

1. Be vigilant over fulfillment of pious wills (c.1301,2).

2. See to execution of pious wills (c.1302,2).

3. Hear interested parties and finance council before approving placing of money and mobile goods (dowry) in a safe place and investing them (c.1305).

4. Hear finance council and interested parties before reducing burdens from wills equitably if they cannot be fulfilled (not Mass obligations) (c.1310,2).

D. The Bishop as Judge: His Ministry of Justice in the Particular Church

1. General Points on the Bishop's Judicial Role (Nonpenal Arena)

a. *Rights of Bishops*
1. Competent to function as judge in all nonreserved cases (c.1419,1).
* 2. Free to commit more significant or more difficult cases to college of three-five judges (c.1425,2).
3. Hear exception of favoritism against officialis or vicar judicial (c.1449,2).
* 4. Authorize gathering of proofs in his diocese by judge from outside it (c.1469,2).
5. Intervene in process personally or through delegate in case of deficiency or neglect by representative of juridic person under his authority (c.1480,2).
6. Establish guidelines on judicial expenses including gratuitous patronage (c.1649,1).
* 7. Execute sentence if his tribunal is first instance court (c.1653,1).
* 8. Decree separation of spouses or permit them to approach civil court (c.1692).
9. Prohibit marriage of one whose first instance annulment has been confirmed in second instance (c.1684,1).
10. Issue declaration of freedom to marry after there is moral certitude of death of first spouse (c.1707,1-2).
11. Challenge validity of ordination if one is the proper ordinary of the individual or the ordinary of place of ordination (c.1708) (*ius*).
*12. Establish office or council to mediate disputes in diocese (c.1733,2).

b. *Responsibilities of Bishops*
1. Strive to avoid contentions arising within the

People of God and settle them amicably as soon as possible (c.1446,1).

* 2. Prepare votum to accompany tribunal votum in transition from nullity case to nonconsummation process (c.1681).

* 3. Transmit own votum and votum of the defender of the bond to the Holy See in nonconsummation cases (c.1705,1).

* 4. Supply additional data to the Holy See in nonconsummation cases (c.1705,2).

2. The Bishop's Ministry of Justice and Pastoral Charity in Penal Matters

a. Rights of Bishops

1. Penalize religious in those instances in which they are subject to him (c.1320).

2. Approve penalty requiring cleric to live in his territory (c.1337,2).

3. Issue warning or rebuke if warranted and specify penance as well (cc.1339; 1340,3).

4. Use other pastoral measures or penal remedies if alleged culprit is acquitted or if no penalty is imposed even if person is guilty of Church offense (c.1348).

5. Remit penalty established by law if one is the ordinary who inflicted or declared it or the ordinary of the place where culprit lives (c.1355,1).

6. Remit nondeclared *latae sententiae* penalty for subjects, those in territory or those who committed Church offense there (c.1355,2).

7. Remit penalty established by precept other than Holy See precept if one is the ordinary of residence of the offender or the ordinary who inflicted or declared penalty (c.1356,1).

8. Issue decree on penal procedure if warranted and indicate whether judicial or administrative procedure is to be followed unless judicial process is required (c.1718,1), e.g., perpetual penalty such as dismissal from the clerical state (c.1342,2).

9. Take certain measures against accused individual, e.g., prohibition against exercising order, prescribed residence in a certain place, etc. (c.1722).

10. Request or approve renunciation of penal process (c.1724,1).

b. Responsibilities of Bishops

* 1. Name priest as canon penitentiary with ordinary nondelegable power to absolve in the sacramental forum from nondeclared *latae sententiae* censures (c.508).

* 2. See to uniformity in penal discipline as much as possible in collaboration with neighboring bishops (c.1316).

3. Use penal procedure (administrative or judicial) only as a last resort; only after all other measures have failed to deal with a problem (c.1341).

4. Provide appropriate support for penalized cleric (unless dismissed) (c.1350,1).

5. Provide as best as one can even for dismissed cleric if he is truly needy (c.1350,2).

6. If one is the ordinary of the residence of the offender, consult the ordinary inflicting or declaring penalty before remitting it if at all possible (c.1355,1).

7. Consult author of precept before remitting penalty attached to its violation unless extraordinary circumstances preclude this (c.1355,2).

8. Make cautious inquiry about probability of Church offense (c.1717,1).

9. Revoke or change decree authorizing penal procedure if such a change is warranted (c.1718,2).

10. Hear two judges or other legal experts if appropriate before issuing decree authorizing penal procedure (c.1718,3).

11. Determine whether possible damages suffered by an aggrieved party could be repaired without formal penal procedure (c.1718,4).

12. Fulfill various responsibilities in an administrative penal procedure (c.1720), e.g., provide appropriate right of defense for accused, consider proofs and arguments with assessors, formulate reasoned decree in light of law and facts.

13. Forward acts to promoter of justice for preparation of libellus if judicial procedure is called for (c.1721,1).

V. The Bishop in His Relationship to Various Members of the People of God

---

A. General Points on the Christian Faithful

1. Preliminary Notions:

1) *Notion of Church member*: one who is incorporated into the Church of Christ through baptism is at the same time constituted a person with all the duties and rights proper to Christians in light of one's condition to the extent that one is in ecclesiastical communion and not subject to a legitimate sanction (c.96).

2) *Notion of Christian faithful* (applicable to laity, clerics and religious): one who is incorporated into Christ by baptism and constituted as part of the People of God; consonant with one's proper juridical condition, such a one participates in a distinctive way in the priestly, prophetic and kingly work of Christ and is called to exercise the mission which God has entrusted to his Church to fulfill in the world (c.204,1).

3) *Notion of one in full communion*: one who is baptized and joined with Christ in visible fellowship by the bonds of profession of faith, sacraments and ecclesiastical government (c.205).

2. Basic Rights and Responsibilities of the Christian Faithful:

a. *Rights:*

1) All Christian Faithful:

1. Enjoy fundamental equality in dignity and action rooted in baptism in virtue of which all are to cooperate in building the Body of Christ

according to their proper condition and responsibility (c.208).

2. Work together that the divine message of salvation may reach more and more effectively all persons at all times everywhere (c.211).

3. Make known to their pastors their wishes and needs, especially spiritual ones (c.212,2).

4. According to their knowledge, competence and position, express to their pastors their opinions on things pertaining to the good of the Church and make them known to other members of the Christian faithful, while showing concern for the integrity of faith and morals and due respect for their pastors with due regard for the common good and the dignity of persons (c.212,3).

5. Be aided by their pastors through the spiritual goods of the Church, especially the word of God and the sacraments (c.213).

6. Worship God according to their own approved rite, and follow their own form of spiritual life, consonant with Church teachings (c.214).

7. Freely found and supervise associations for the purpose of charity or piety or to foster the Christian vocation in the world; hold meetings for these purposes (c.215; cc.298-329).

8. Share in the Church's mission and initiate on their own projects for promoting and sustaining apostolic activity. (No one, however can claim the name *Catholic* without the consent of the proper authority.) (c.216)

9. Receive a Christian education, a knowledge of the mystery of salvation and instruction in right living, appropriate to one's maturity (c.217).

10. Choose a state of life, free from all coercion (c.219).

11. Enjoy a good reputation which no one may harm illegitimately (c.220).

12. Vindicate and defend their rights in a competent ecclesiastical forum according to the norm of law (c.221,1).

13. Be judged by the prescriptions of law applied with equity (c.221,2).

14. Not be punished except according to the norm of law (c.221,3).

2) **All Christian Faithful Engaged in the Pursuit of the Sacred Sciences**
Enjoy freedom of inquiry and expression in those matters in which they are competent with due regard for the magisterium of the Church (c.218).

3) **General Principle on the Exercise of Rights**
The Christian faithful can exercise their rights individually or in associations, taking into account the common good of the Church, the rights of others, and one's duties toward others. Ecclesiastical authority is competent to moderate the exercise of the above rights in view of the common good (c.223).

b. *Responsibilities:*

1. Maintain communion with the Church in their activity (c.209,1).

2. Diligently fulfill their duties toward the universal Church and the particular church to which they belong (c.209,2).

3. Lead a holy life, promoting the Church's growth and sanctification (c.210).

4. Work together that the divine message of salvation may reach more and more effectively all persons at all times everywhere (c.211).

5. Follow teachings and rulings of the bishops as representatives of Christ with due awareness of their own responsibility (c.212,1).

6. According to their knowledge, competence and position, express to their pastors their opinion on things pertaining to the good of the Church and make it known to other members of the Christian faithful with due regard for the common good and the dignity of persons (c.212,3).

7. Provide for the needs of the Church so that what is needed for divine worship, apostolic works, charity and a just sustenance for its ministers will be available (c.222,1).

8. Promote social justice and aid the poor from their own resources, mindful of the precept of the Lord (c.222,2).

B. The Bishop in His Relationship to the Laity

1. Description of Laypersons:

Laypersons are deputed to the apostolate by baptism and confirmation, participate in the saving mission of the Church and take on a specific work, especially that of bearing witness to Christ in the ordering of temporal matters and secular affairs in accord with the Gospel (c.225). They are differentiated by divine institution from sacred ministers called clerics (c.207,1).

2. Basic Rights, Aptitudes and Responsibilities of All Laypersons:

a. Rights:

1) Work as individuals or in associations that the divine message of salvation may be made known and accepted by all persons everywhere in the world (c.225,1).

2) Enjoy civil liberty proper to all citizens (c.227).

3) Acquire a profound knowledge of Christian teaching appropriate to their capacity and condition so that in exercising their part in the apostolate they may live it, proclaim it and, if necessary, defend it (c.229,1).

4) Acquire a profound knowledge of the sacred sciences, attend ecclesiastical universities and schools of religious studies and receive academic degrees (c.229,2).

5) Receive a fitting and proportionate remuneration to provide for themselves and their families, and, to the extent that it can be provided, social security and health insurance if they permanently or temporarily give themselves to a special service of the Church (c.231,2).

b. Aptitudes (Not Strict Rights but General Christian Competency to Assume Various Tasks):

1) Be called by pastors of the Church to ecclesiastical offices and tasks in accord with the law given requisite qualifications (c.228,1).

2) Assist pastors of the Church as experts and coun-

selors even in councils in accord with the law if the laypersons in question are outstanding as regards the requisite knowledge, prudence and honesty (c.228,2).

3) Receive a mandate to teach the sacred sciences from legitimate ecclesiastical authority if they are qualified in accord with the law (c.229,3).

4) Be deputed temporarily to serve as lectors and enjoy the faculty of serving as commentators and cantors and fulfilling other functions according to the norm of law (c.230,2).

5) In cases of need when there are no sacred ministers, supply for these offices by exercising the ministry of the Word, presiding at liturgical prayer, conferring baptism and distributing communion (c.230,3).

c. Responsibilities:

1) Work as an individual or in associations that the divine message of salvation may be made known and accepted by all persons everywhere in the world. This duty is all the more urgent in situations where people can hear the Gospel and know Christ only through laypersons (c.225,1).

2) In exercising their right to civil liberty, take care that their actions are imbued with the spirit of the Gospel and that they direct their attention to the teaching of the magisterium while avoiding proposing their own opinions as Church teaching in debatable matters (c.227).

3) Acquire a knowledge of Christian teaching so that in exercising their part in the apostolate they may live it, proclaim it, and, if necessary, defend it (c.229,1).

4) Be properly formed for their work if they permanently or temporarily give themselves to a special service of the Church (c.231,1).

3. Specific Rights, Aptitudes and Responsibilities of Certain Laypersons:

a. Laymen:

If qualified, they have the aptitude to be installed permanently in the ministries of lector and acolyte;

however this does not confer the right to sustenance or remuneration from the Church (c.230,1).

b. Married Persons:

1) Laypersons who are married have a vocation and a responsibility to work for the building up of the People of God through marriage and the family (c.226,1).

2) Parents especially have the most serious duty and right to educate their children and to teach them according to the doctrine of the Church (c.226,2).

4. Brief Summary of Nonordained Ministries for Which Laypersons Are Competent:

a)   Reception of mandate to teach theology and other sacred sciences (c.229,3)

b)   Acolyte if layman (c.230,1)

c)   Formal installation as lector if layman (c.230,1); temporary deputation as lector if layman or laywoman (c.230,2)

d)   Chancellor (c.483,2) at least as regards archival responsibilities in cc.482-491 as distinct from frequent U.S. practice of delegating episcopal faculties to such an officer

e)   Notary except in case involving possible jeopardizing of priest's reputation (c.483,2)

f)   Diocesan fiscal officer (c.494)

g)   Member of diocesan or parish finance council (cc.492-493; 537)

h)   Member of diocesan or parish pastoral council if it is established (cc.512,1; 536)

i)   Participation in exercise of leadership role in a parish under supervision of a priest (c.517,2)

j)   Preaching in a non-Eucharistic setting; homily at Eucharist is reserved to priests and deacons (cc.766; 767,1)

k)   Missionary (c.784)

l)   Catechist (c.785)

m) Extraordinary minister of baptism (c.861,2)

n)   Extraordinary minister of Eucharist (c.910,2)

o)   Deputation as extraordinary minister of exposition of Blessed Sacrament (c.943)

p)   Delegation to assist at weddings after bishop is

authorized to do so by conference of bishops and Holy See (c.1112)

q) Judge in collegiate tribunal with two clerics after bishop is authorized by conference of bishops (c.1421,2)

r) Assessor (c.1424)

s) Auditor (c.1428,2)

t) Promoter of justice (c.1435)

u) Defender of bond (c.1435)

v) Procurator-advocate (c.1483)

w) Legal expert in difficult non-consummation cases (c.1701,2)

C. The Bishop in His Relationship to Clerics

N.B. The focus here is on the bishop in his rapport with individual priests as distinct from corporate groups such as presbyteral councils.

The bishop is to be especially concerned about priests and listen to them as his assistants and advisers. He is to protect their rights and see to it that they correctly fulfill the obligations proper to their state. He is also to see to it that means and institutions are available to them to foster their spiritual and intellectual life. He is also to make provision for their decent support and social assistance in accord with the norm of law (c.384).

1. Rights of Bishops

* 1. Issue letter of incardination or excardination for cleric (c.267,1).

* 2. Recall cleric who has migrated to another particular church (c.271,3).

3. Expect cleric to show reverence and obedience (c.273).

4. Ordinarily expect cleric to accept assignment (c.274,2).

5. Possibly issue norms fostering desirable clerical collaboration in achieving mission of Church (c.275,1).

6. Possibly issue norms on clergy retreats (c.276,2,4°).

7. Possibly issue norms regarding problematic clerical friendships and make decisions on such in individual cases (c.277,3).

8. Possibly issue norms on continuing clerical education (c.279,2) (reference to particular law).

9. Permit cleric to depart from diocese for a notable time (c.283,1).

10. Possibly issue norms on things to be avoided as unbecoming a cleric (c.285,1) (reference to particular law).

11. Permit assumption of various administrative responsibilities by cleric (c.285,4).

12. Permit cleric to engage in businesses or trade (c.286) (reference to 'legitimate ecclesiastical authority').

13. Authorize active clerical involvement in partisan political activity or union activity if protection of rights of Church or fostering common good require it (c.287,2) (reference to 'competent ecclesiastical authority').

14. Permit cleric to enter military service voluntarily (c.289,1).

15. Authorize cleric not to take advantage of exemption in civil law from duties incompatible with the clerical state (c.289,2).

2. Responsibilities of Bishops

* 1. Express mind regarding request of cleric for *ipso iure* incardination after five years in another diocese if one is the cleric's proper bishop or the bishop of the other diocese; this expression of intent is to be done in writing within four months of the cleric's request (c.268,1).

* 2. Meet certain conditions before cleric from another diocese is incardinated, e.g., ascertain that such a move is for the good of the diocese and that the cleric can be supported, obtain letter of excardination from cleric's bishop as well as testimonials about his good character, obtain written declaration of cleric's intent to serve in new diocese (c.269).

* 3. Grant excardination of cleric for a just cause; deny excardination of cleric only for a just cause (c.270).

* 4. Not deny permission to migrate to a cleric especially to a diocese short of clergy; work out arrangement with the bishop of that other diocese regarding the rights and obligations of the migrating cleric (c.271,1).

* 5. Observe justice and natural equity and written agreements with bishop of other diocese in recalling cleric who has migrated (c.271,3).

6. Respect clerical right to join with others in pursuit of goals in keeping with clerical state (c.278,1).

7. Encourage secular priests' associations, which among

other things foster better relationships with bishops (c.278,2).

8. Provide for continuing education courses and conferences for clerics in view of enhancing their theological-pastoral knowledge (c.279,2).

9. Respect clerical right to adequate income in remuneration for fulfillment of ecclesial ministry (c.281,1).

10. Respect clerical right to social assistance and provide for their needs in time of illness, incapacity or old age (c.281,2).

11. Respect right of married deacons devoting themselves full time to Church service to adequate remuneration for themselves and their families (c.281,3).

12. Respect clerical right to a reasonable period of vacation, i.e., one month for pastors and associates (cc.283,2; 533,2; 550,3).

D. The Bishop in His Relationship to Religious

From both of these groups, clerics and laypersons, there are Christian faithful who by vow or other bond, recognized and ratified by the Church, profess the evangelical counsels and are consecrated in a special way to God. (These persons are commonly known as *religious*.) (c.207,2)

1. Rights of Bishops

1. For serious reasons suppress associations established by religious with approval of the bishop (c.320,2)(cf.c.312,2).

* 2. Determine how religious representatives at a diocesan synod are to be chosen (c.463,1,9°).

* 3. Determine how religious representatives to diocesan pastoral council are to be chosen (c.512,1).

* 4. Entrust a parish to religious (c.520).

5. Name chaplain for a lay institute (c.567,1).

* 6. Establish a religious community in his diocese (c.579).

* 7. If one is the bishop of the diocese where the principal house of a diocesan religious community is located, exercise supervisory role over such a community, e.g., approve constitutions, confirm changes unless Holy See

has intervened, deal with major issues exceeding competence of internal religious authority (c.595,1).

* 8. Dispense from the constitutions of diocesan communities in individual cases (c.595,2).
* 9. Receive profession of evangelical counsels of hermit and guide hermit's life (c.603,2).
10. Consecrate virgins according to liturgical rite (c.604).
*11. Approve in writing establishment of religious house in diocese (c.609,1).
*12. Approve in writing the establishment of a monastery of nuns (moniales) in his diocese (c.609,2) (Holy See approval also necessary).
*13. Approve change in apostolic orientation of a religious house in diocese (c.612).
*14. Exercise a supervisory role over an autonomous monastery in a diocese (c.615).
*15. Be consulted regarding the suppression of a religious house in his diocese (c.616,1).
*16. Preside at election of the superiors of autonomous monasteries (c.625,2).
*17. Visit autonomous monasteries and diocesan religious communities (c.628,2) (ius).
18. Approve confessors for nuns (moniales), houses of formation and lay communities (c.630,3).
19. Receive financial report from autonomous monasteries once a year; be informed of financial situation of a diocesan religious community (c.637) (ius).
20. Approve alienation of property of autonomous monastery and of diocesan religious community (c.638,4).
21. Be consulted before secular cleric is admitted to a religious community (c.644).
22. Issue testimonials for secular cleric or one in seminary to enter a religious community (c.645,2).
*23. Enter cloister of nuns (moniales) for just cause and permit them to leave or others to enter cloister for a serious reason (c.667,4).
24. Expect religious to be properly deferential in matters of apostolate, pastoral care and public worship (c.678,1).
*25. Prohibit individual religious from remaining in diocese if superior does not take appropriate action (c.679).
*26. Supervise apostolic works entrusted to religious (c.681,1).
*27. Appoint religious to a diocesan office (c.682,1).
*28. Remove religious from diocesan office (c.682,2).

*29. Visit churches, oratories that believers frequent often, schools (not those for members of religious community alone) and other spiritual or temporal works of religion run by religious (c.683,1).

*30. Deal with abuses in religious institution if superior fails to do so (c.683,2).

31. Approve decree of exclaustration for priest living in his diocese; extend such an indult beyond three years in the case of a religious in a diocesan community or grant such an extended indult initially (c.686,1).

*32. Impose exclaustration on a member of a diocesan community for serious reasons at the request of the supreme moderator with the consent of the council (c.686,3).

33. Exclaustrated cleric subject to pastoral care of and dependent on local ordinary (c.687).

*34. Confirm indult of departure for serious reasons of one in temporary profession in diocesan communities or in autonomous monastery (c.688,2).

*35. Grant indult of departure for one in perpetual vows in a diocesan community (c.691,2).

*36. Incardinate or receive experimentally priest granted indult of departure from religious community (so-called 'benevolent bishop' in law) (c.693).

*37. Grant dismissal of one in an autonomous monastery (c.699,2).

*38. Confirm decree of dismissal before it is executed in reference to member of autonomous monastery or diocesan community (c.700).

*39. Grant indult of departure for perpetually incorporated member of a diocesan secular institute (c.727,1).

*40. Approve establishment of house of society of apostolic life; be consulted before it is suppressed (c.733,1).

41. Expect members of societies of apostolic life to be duly deferential in matters of divine worship, pastoral care and apostolate (c.738,2).

42. Approve living arrangement for definitively incorporated member of society of apostolic life wishing to live outside it for three years (c.745).

*43. Call religious to aid in announcing the Gospel (c.758).

*44. Approve schools operated by religious (c.801).

*45. Supervise schools in dioceses including those run by

religious; issue norms on general organization of schools (c.806,1) (*ius*).

46. Authorize cleric or religious to publish in journals generally contrary to faith and morals (c.831,1).

*47. Approve religious building a church even if he has approved establishment of religious house (c.1215,3).

48. Prescribe special collection to be taken up even in churches of religious (c.1266).

49. Oversee activity of religious who is a trustee vis-à-vis goods destined for diocese (c.1302,3).

50. Penalize religious in those instances in which they are subject to him (c.1320).

2. Responsibilities of Bishops

1. Hear moderator and major officers before suppressing public association established by religious through apostolic indult with bishop's approval (c.320,3).

* 2. Obtain approval of the religious superior before entrusting a parish to religious (c.520,1).

* 3. Consult Holy See before establishing religious community in diocese (c.579).

4. Protect and guard autonomy of religious communities (c.586,2).

5. Respect implications of exemption of religious from authority of local ordinaries (c.591).

* 6. Manifest special care for diocesan communities (c.594).

* 7. Consult other bishops in dioceses where a diocesan community has houses in various aspects of exercising supervisory role over them (c.595,1).

* 8. Discern new forms of consecrated life and aid founders in expressing their insights and protecting them with appropriate statutes (c.605).

* 9. Visit autonomous monasteries and diocesan communities (c.628,2).

10. Consult communities before approving confessor (c.630.3).

*11. Obtain approval of the superior for nuns (*moniales*) to leave cloister or for others to enter (c.667,4).

12. Encourage observance of religious rule amid apostolic activity (c.678,2).

*13. Consult religious superiors regarding community involvement in various apostolic enterprises (c.678,3).

*14. Refer to Holy See case of religious prohibited from

being in diocese if religious superior takes no action (c.679).

15. Foster secular-religious apostolic collaboration (c.680).

*16. Take cognizance of rights of religious superiors in supervising apostolic works entrusted to religious (c.681,1).

*17. Elicit presentation by or at least approval of religious superior before religious is given a diocesan appointment (c.682,1).

*18. Advise religious superior about certain problems to be dealt with in connection with episcopal visitation (c.683,2).

19. Exercise pastoral care in relationship to exclaustrated cleric (c.687).

*20. Take appropriate action within five years to deny incardination of religious cleric received experimentally after indult of departure from religious community; otherwise he is automatically incardinated after five years (c.693).

*21. Review acts of council, which have been forwarded by religious superior in case of dismissal from an autonomous monastery (c.699,2).

E. The Bishop in His Relationship to Those Not Fully in Communion with the Catholic Church

1. Rights of Bishops

1. Establish norms on ecumenical matters in light of directives of supreme Church authority (c.755,2).

* 2. Judge when a 'grave necessity' warrants authorizing Western Christians not in full communion to receive penance, anointing and Eucharist (conference of bishops may also make such a determination) (c.844,4).

3. Authorize celebration of Eucharist in a non-Catholic church (c.933).

4. Dispense from impediment of disparity of worship and permit marriage of Catholic and baptized non-Catholic under certain conditions (c.1125).

5. If the local ordinary of the Catholic party, dispense from canonical form in mixed marriages (c.1127,2).

6. Permit Catholic burial service for unbaptized infant or member of other Christian church (c.1183,2-3).

2. Responsibilities of Bishops

1. Be solicitous for welfare of various groups including baptized and nonbaptized non-Catholics (c.383).

2. Foster ecumenical movement and establish norms in light of directive of supreme Church authority (c.755,2).

3. Consult with hierarchs of other communions before policy on sacramental sharing is articulated (c.844,5).

4. See to fulfillment of conditions/*cautiones* before permission is granted for mixed marriage (c.1125).

5. Consult the local ordinary of the place of marriage if different from the local ordinary of the Catholic party before dispensation from form is granted (c.1127,2).

6. Support couples involved in ecumenical marriages (c.1128).

Index

Abduction, as impediment to marriage, 13
Abortion, as irregularity for orders, 9, 10
Absolution, general conditions for, 7, 8, 35
Abuses in religious institutions, 69
Administration, extraordinary acts of, 35
  ministry of bishop in, 36-56
Administrative decree, 36
  data-gathering and consultation, 36
  interpretation, 37
  issuance in writing, 36
  time for issuing, 36
  validity, 37
Administrative oversight re: public juridic persons, 53
Administrative responsibilities, 66
Administrator of diocese, election of, 33
Administrator of temporalities, bishop as, 52-56
Administrator, parish, 50, 51
  appointment, 50
  description, 50
  qualifications, 50
  responsibilities, 50, 51
Advocate, 46
  appointment, 46
  description, 46
  duration of office, 46
  qualifications, 46
Affinity, as impediment to marriage, 13
Age of sponsor for baptism, 6
Agreement with another bishop re: status of migrating cleric, 12
Alienation of Church goods, 43, 53
Alienation of property of diocese, 33, 43, 54, 55
Announcing of Gospel, exercise of, moderation of, 24
Anointing of sick, 8, 35
Apostasy as irregularity for orders, dispensation from, 9, 10, 11

Apostolic collaboration of seculars and religious, 71
Apostolic works entrusted to religious, supervision of, 68
Aptitude for ordination, 9
Assignment, acceptance of by cleric, 65
Associate pastor, see Vicar, parish
Association, right of, for clerics, 66
Associations established by religious, suppression of, 67
Associations of priests, encouragement of, 66
Attempted marriage as irregularity for orders, 9, 10, 11
Attempted suicide as irregularity for orders, 10, 11
Auditor, 45
  appointment, 45
  description, 45
  qualifications, 45
Authenticity of prayer, and pious practices, vigilance over, 6
Authority, legislative of bishop, those subject to, 27, 28
Autonomy of religious communities, protection of, 70
Auxiliary bishop, 37, 38

Baptism, 6
  in hospital, 6
  in private home, 6
  minister extraordinary, deputation of those over 16, 6
  minister ordinary, function as, 6
Bination, 7
Bishop, coadjutor and auxiliary, 37
  appointment, 37
  status, 38
  taking possession, 38
Bishop, consecration of, 11
  proper for ordination, 8
Blessing of church, 17
  of oils, 5
  of sacred places, 17
Books, approval of, 23

censors of, 23
liturgical, approval of, 23
translation of, 23
prayer, approval of, 23
Building of church,
approval of, 18, 32
by religious, 18
Burial, 17
in doubtful cases, 17
norms on, 36
of non-Catholics, 17, 72
of unbaptized infant, 17, 72
Business or trade, exercise of by
clerics or religious, 66

Candidacy for ordination, 9
Canonical form of marriage, dispensation from, 71
Canon penitentiary, 58
Capital, excess, investment of, 53
Catechetical activity, norms on, 22, 24
Catechetical resources, availability of, 24
Catechetical responsibility, 24
Catechetical undertaking, coordination of, 24
Catechisms, approval of, 23
preparation of, 24
Catechists, formation and continuing education of, 24
Cautiones for mixed marriage, 14
Celebret, 7
Cemeteries, establishment of, 18
Censors of books, choice of, 23
Certificate of ordination, 12
Chair of theology in Catholic universities, establishment of, 25
Chancellor, 41, 42
appointment, 41
description, 41
duration of office, 42
loss of office, 42
qualifications, 41
Change in apostolic orientation of religious house, 68
Chapel, private, erection of, 18
sacred functions permitted in, 18
Chaplain for houses of lay religious institutes, 67
Chrism, consecration of, 6
Christian faithful, 59-61
be judged by prescriptions of law applied with equity, 60
description of, 59
enjoy good reputation, 60
express opinion on issues affecting the Church, 60, 61

follow own form of spiritual life, 60
follow teaching and rulings of bishops, 61
found and moderate associations and hold meetings, 60
freely choose state of life, 60
lead a holy life, 61
make known spiritual needs, 60
promote social justice, 61
receive a Christian education, 60
receive spiritual goods of the Church, 60
responsibilities of, 61
rights of, 59-61
share in the Church's mission, 60
support the Church, 61
vindicate and defend rights in ecclesiastical forum, 60
work to realize divine plan of salvation, 60, 61
worship God according to proper rite, 60
Church
blessing of, 17
building of, approval of, 18, 32
building of by religious, approval of, 18
conversion to secular purposes, approval of, 18, 32
Civil law exemptions of cleric, 66
problems posed by marriage, 13
Civil litigation, approval of administrators engaging in, 53
Cleric, 65-67
acceptance of assignment, 65
assumption of administrative responsibilities, 66
civil law exemptions, 66
continuing education of, norms on, 35, 65, 67
dismissal, provision for, 49, 58
engaging in business or trade, 66
engaging in partisan political activity or union activity, 66
entering military service, 66
exclaustration of, 69
holding of public office, 10
inappropriate activity of, 35
migrating to another church, recall of, 12, 65, 66
problematic friendship of, 65
reverence for and obedience to ordinary, 65
right, of association, 66

74

to adequate income, 67
to social assistance, 67
to vacation, 35, 67
Cleric secular, admission to religious community, 68
Clerical behavior, supervision of, 34
Cloister of nuns, 68
departure from, 68
entrance into, 68
Coadjutor, 37, 38
Collaboration apostolic, of seculars and religious, 71
Collection, special even in churches of religious, 70
College of consultors, 32, 33
description, 32, 33
functions, 33
College students, pastoral care of, 25
Commentator, lay person as, 63
Commitment to ecclesial service, reception of, 9
to ordination, 9
Communion full, notion of, 59
responsibilities of one in, 61
rights of one in, 59-61
Community, diocesan, consultation with other bishops, 70
re: dispensation from constitutions of, 68
Community religious in diocese, establishment of, 68
Community religious in diocese, exercise of supervisory role over, 67
Conditional marriage, permission of, 14
Confessions, faculties for, 8
granting of, 8
revocation of, 8
hearing of personally, 7
[see also Penance]
Confessors for nuns, lay communities and houses of formation, 68
Confirmation, minister ordinary, 6
determination of age for, 6
function as ordinary minister of, 6
outside diocese, 7
priests associated in administration on an *ad hoc* basis, 6
priests empowered to administer, 6
reasonable request for, 7
within diocese, 6
Conjugal separation, 15, 16
Conjugicide, as impediment to marriage, 13

Consanguinity, as impediment to marriage, 13
Consecration of bishop, 11
of oils, 5
Consecrations, reserved, 16
Constitutions of diocesan communities, dispensation from, 68
Consultation with expert re: exercise of orders, 10, 12
Consultation with finance council, 42
Consultation with judges or experts re: penal procedure, 58
Consultation with leaders of other churches, 72
Consultation with other bishops re: diocesan communities, 70
general absolution, 35
Consultation with presbyteral council, 32, 33, 55
Consultation with religious superiors re: apostolic involvement, 70
Consultors, college of, 32, 33
Continuing education of catechists, 24
of cleric, 35, 65, 67
Convalidation of marriage, 15, 16
Conversion of church to secular purposes, 18, 32
of sacred places to secular purpose, 18
Council, diocesan pastoral
[see Diocesan pastoral council]
Council, episcopal
[see Episcopal council]
Council, finance
[see Finance council]
Council, presbyteral
[see Presbyteral council]
Cult of saints, sacred images and relics, 17
Curia, diocesan, general rules on, 39
moderator of, 40
Custom, 28, 29

Damages, settlement of without penal procedure, 58
Deacon, 9, 12
internship, time for, 9
ordination of, 9
priestly ordination, refusal of by, 12
prohibition of exercise of orders for one refusing priestly ordination, 12
Deacon married, right to adequate remuneration, 67

75

illegitimate exercise of ministry, 10

illegitimate reception of orders, 11

marriage, 10

neophyte, 11

office demanding civil accountability, 10, 11

psychic disorder, 9

Impotence, as impediment to marriage, 13

Inappropriate activity of cleric, 35

Incardination, 33, 65, 66, 69

conditions for, 66

ipso iure, 66

letter of, 65, 66

Income adequate, right to, 67

Indult of departure, 69

Inquiry, freedom of, 61

Inquiry re: probability of offense, 58

Insanity as irregularity for orders, 11

Institutes of higher religious studies, establishment of, 25

Instruction of candidates for ordination, 12

Interdicted person, marriage of, 13

Interpellations, 15

dispensation from, 15

of convert before baptism, 15

Investment of excess capital, 53

Irregularity for orders, dispensation from, 9, 10, 11

[see also Impediment to orders]

abortion, 9, 10

apostasy, 9, 10, 11

attempted marriage, 9, 10, 11

attempted suicide, 10, 11

heresy, 9, 10, 11

homicide, 9, 10

illegitimate positing of act of orders, 10, 11

illegitimate reception of orders, 11

insanity, 11

mutilation of another, 10, 11

psychic disorder, 9, 10, 11, 12

schism, 9, 10, 11

self-mutilation, 10, 11

Journals contrary to faith and morals, approval of publication in, 23, 70

Judge, bishop as, 56-58

Judge, 44, 45

appointment, 44

description, 44

duration of office, 45

qualifications, 44

Judicial expenses, guidelines on, 56

Juridic person, acceptance of foundation by, 36, 54

Justice, promoter of, 45, 58

Laity, authorization to assist at marriage, 14

Lay communities, confessors for, 68

Lay institute, appointment of chaplain of, 67

Laymen, aptitude for certain nonordained ministries, 64-65

Layperson, 62-65

aptitude for various tasks, 62-63

assistance to bishop as expert and counsellor, 62-63

call to ecclesiastical offices, 62

custody of Eucharist by, 7

function as lector, commentator, 63

mission to teach sacred sciences, 63

responsibilities of, 63

acquire knowledge of Christian teaching, 63

be properly formed for Church service, 63

reflect spirit of Gospel and magisterial teaching in actions, 63

work for realization of divine plan, 63

rights of, 62

acquire knowledge of Christian teaching, 62

attend ecclesiastical universities and schools of religious studies, 62

enjoy civil liberty, 62

receive fitting and proportionate remuneration, 62

work for realization of divine plan, 62

summary of options for exercise of nonordained ministries, 64-65

supply for sacred ministers in various offices, 63

Leaders of other churches, consultation with, 72

Lector, layperson as, 63

Legal relationship, as impediment to marriage, 13

Legislation particular, types of, 27, 28, 34

78

Legislative authority of bishop,
those subject to, 27, 28
Ligamen, as impediment to marriage, 13
Litigation civil, approval of administrators engaging in, 53
Liturgical books, approval of, 23
translation of, approval of, 23
Liturgical celebrations, personally
preside at, 6
Liturgical life, moderation of, 5

Mandate papal, required for episcopal ordination, 11
Mandate papal, required to ordain
Oriental rite candidate, 11
Mandate papal, required to send
dimissorials to bishop of other
rite, 12
Mandate to teach theological disciplines, 22, 23
Marriage, 12-16
as impediment to orders, dispensation from, 10
attempted as irregularity for orders, dispensation from, 9,
10
authorization of laity to assist
at, 14
authorization of priests or deacons to assist at, 14
by proxy, 13
conditional, 14
convalidation of, 15, 16
dispensation from canonical
form of, 71
dispensation from impediments
in danger of death, 14
impediments to, 13-14
in presumed death case, 56
mixed, 13, 14, 16, 72
of interdicted person, 13
of minors, 13
of one who has notoriously
abandoned the Church, 13
of those subject to an interdict,
13
of those who are excommunicated, 13
of those who are migrants, 13
of those who have obligations
from a prior marriage, 13
of those whose marriage poses
civil law problems, 13
outside of Church, permission
of, 14
personal assistance at, 14
registration of in case of dispensation from form, 14

sanation of, 15
secret, 16
secret, permission of, 15
temporary prohibition of, 13
to non-Catholic by one using
Pauline privilege, 15
Married couples, organization of
pastoral care of, 15
rights and responsibilities of, 64
spiritual enrichment of, 15
Mass obligations, reduction of, 54
surplus, reception of, 7
transferral of, 54
vigilance in fulfillment of, 7
Maturity of candidate for ordination, 9
Media, approval of, 23
education of faithful in use of,
25
Media, use of in teaching, 25
Mediation, office or council of, 56
Member of Church, notion of, 59
Migrating cleric
agreement with another bishop
re: status of, 12
in another church, 65, 66
Migrants and diocesan laws, 28
marriage of, 13
Military service, cleric entering, 66
Minimum age for ordination, dispensation from, 9
Ministry, illegitimate exercise of as
impediment to orders, 10
Ministry of bishop, in administration, 36-56
judging, 56-58
sanctifying, 5-19
Ministry team
[see Team ministry]
Minors, marriage of, 13
Missa pro populo, 6
Mission parish, norms on, 35
Missionary enterprise, solicitude
about, 24
Mixed marriage, permission of, 13,
14, 72
Mixed marriage, support of couples in, 16, 72
Moderator of curia, 40
appointment, 40
description, 40
qualifications, 40
Moderator of team ministry, 50
Monastery autonomous in diocese,
68
alienation of property, 68
confirm decree of dismissal of
member, 69

dismissal of one in, 69
financial report, 68
preside at election of superior, 68
supervisory role over, 68
visitation of, 68
Monastery of nuns, establishment of, 68
Mutilation
of another as irregularity for orders, 10, 11
self as irregularity for orders, 10, 11

Negligence, administrative, 48, 53
Negligence, administrative by representative of juridic person, 56
Nonbaptized, preaching of Gospel to, 24
Non-Catholic Christians, sacramental sharing with, 6, 35, 71
Non-Catholic church, celebration of Eucharist in, 71
Nonconsummation votum, preparation of and transmission to Holy See, 57
Nonordained ministries, aptitude of laymen for, 64-65
Notary, 42
appointment, 42
description, 42
duration of office, 42
qualifications, 42
Notification of parish of baptism re: ordination, 12
Notorious ex-Catholic, marriage of, 13
Nuns, cloister of, 68
confessors for, 68
establishment of monastery of, 68

Obedience of clergy to ordinary, 65
Observance of religious rule, 70
Offense, inquiry re: probability of, 58
Offerings, parish, 34
Office, civil forbidden to clerics as impediment to orders, dispensation from, 10
Officialis
[see Vicar judicial]
Oils, consecration or blessing of, 5
Omnia parata situation, dispensation from marriage impediment, 14
Oratory, approval of, building of, 18

conversion to secular purposes, 18
forbid functions in, 18
visitation of proposed site of, 19
Orders, 8
as impediment to marriage, 14
consultation with expert re:, 10, 12
dispensation from impediments to, 10-11
exercise of by one with psychic disorder, 9
Ordination, 8-12
aptitude for, 9
candidacy for, 9
certificate of, 12
commitment to, 9
illegitimate reception of, 11
instruction of candidates for, 12
irregularities for and impediments to, 9-11
maturity of candidate, 9
minimum age for, dispensation from, 9
minister ordinary, function as, 8
notification of parish of baptism, 12
outside of one's diocese, permission for, 11
questionable candidate for, 12
readiness for, 9, 12
registration and proof of, 12
retreat before, 9, 12
scrutinies before, means of pursuing, 11, 12
Oriental rite candidate, mandate required for ordination of, 11

Parents, rights and responsibilities of, 64
Parish
administrator, 50-51
entrusted to religious, 67
mission, 35
offerings, 34
pastoral councils, 34
registers, supplementary, 34
vicar, 51
Parochial administrator
[see Administrator, parish]
Particular law, 28-36
areas for, 34-36
types of, 28-29
Parochial vicar
[see Vicar, parish]
Pastor, 46-50
appointment, 47
consultation before appointment, 47

Notes

Notes

Notes

Notes